The Walk-In

Juelle

BookPartners, Inc.
Wilsonville, Oregon

BookPartners, Inc.
P. O. Box 922
Wilsonville, Oregon 97070

Dedication

I dedicate this book to you, the reader, with honor, love and support. Thank you for your precious contribution to this planet's evolutionary transformation.

Acknowledgements

I am eternally grateful to the following people who have influenced the creation of this work:

Donovan, for your infinite love, support and companionship; Christian, for being my favorite "cosmic cheerleader;" Thorn and Ursula Bacon, for seeing my vision and lending your genius in helping me to manifest it; Mary Young, for leaving the voice message on my answering machine that gave me the final nudge; Kathleen Hayes, for gracing my entry with your presence; Sandy Hogan, gifted writer, visionary and manifester of dreams; and finally to "The Council" for illuminating all our pathways home.

Table Of Contents

Prologue

I'm a walk-in. I'm a Spirit who occupies a human body that was host to an original Spirit who departed. You might say I'm an entirely different entity, one who came to dwell in the flesh and experience of another person.

What I've written may startle some people. The idea of a new Spirit occupying the body and assuming the life that previously belonged to another person may seem too incredible to imagine. But there is nothing evil or bewitching about walk-ins. It's a more common phenomenon than one might think. Walk-ins have been coming to Earth since time immemorial. We are just now beginning to make our identities known as we accelerate into the new millennium and the inevitable spiritual awakening of humanity and our planet.

The walk-in experience is concisely demonstrated by a powerful account from one of my favorite spiritual books by Paramahansa Yogananda. This story took place in India many years ago. A young man had recently died and a parade of mourners carried him to his funeral pyre at the cremation grounds. Just as they prepared to light the fire, an old man came running, crying out, "Stop! Don't do it! I can use that body!" As soon as he uttered these words, his frail, aged body crumpled lifeless to the ground. At that moment, the young man sat up, sprang down from the pyre and ran off into the woods. The old man, who was a great saint, was so immersed in sacred communion with God-presence that he didn't want to interrupt his devotions by taking rebirth into an infant's helpless body.

The events of the past five years of my life have prepared me to understand the profound miracle of this story. As a walk-in, I'm a unique Spirit who occupies a human body that was host to another unique Spirit who chose to depart. I'm a new player, who rotated in for the earlier one who rotated out of the earthly game. I'm now wearing her uniform of flesh and blood and life experiences. We agreed long ago, at a soul level, before embodiment, that we would share a uniform in order to play a more accelerated role in human evolution.

Like everyone else, we have volunteered to aid in planetary transformation by assuming a human body. With a slight twist. Since Infinite Wisdom selects the players for the earthly stage who can best perform the tasks to be accomplished, the original inhabitant, the walk-out, reaches a point in his or her Spirit's journey that will benefit by a return to and a renewal of inspiration from Divine Source. The replacement Spirit, the walk-in, assumes this more mature body to forego the long delay of growing from infancy to childhood to adulthood. It's a very efficient "birth" process, one that hermit crabs understand instinctively. They shed their shells as they grow and assume the abandoned shell of another of their species for an interim period, until they grow too large for that "house." And the cycle continues.

There are as many possibilities for a walk-in experience as there are walk-ins themselves. I entered Shari's body when she was 40 years old. She had been "in training" for this event, so to speak, all of her earthly life, even though she never had a conscious inkling that her Spirit would be called to another assignment. She has gone to the light where all souls are re-connected to one another and to the glory of Infinite Oneness.

I had been in training too, although my "earthly" training really started when I was "born" into a fully-functioning, adult, female body and a full life with a history of relationships and responses that I had to assimilate before I could function effectively here in third dimension.

The Walk-In is my personal story, both from Shari's perspective as the walk-out and mine, Juelle's, as the walk-in. We are distinct personalities. Because we have both chosen human embodiment, we have human talents and tastes. The transformation and integration process seemed odd to me, like the discomfort of molding one's feet into the worn imprint of a stranger's shoes. It's bound to be uncomfortable until new imprints are established. For example, I was inconvenienced by the dark emotions that hid among Shari's memories and influenced her behavior. Yet I also inherited the great gifts of her daughter's love and her husband's devotion.

It's a true story. I've told it from my heart and from Shari's heart. Even though she is no longer here, her memories occupy this body down to the tiniest cell. Over the years, the memories that she captured as well as my own have merged, and I am stronger for the union. It is my Spirit who now occupies the body that Shari left behind, but the memory of her is like a soft, permanent shadow that offers me comfort and the rich inheritance of a zest for life.

1

Growing Up Mennonite

Life began for me when fragmented childhood memories finally wove together a pattern that I could call my own. Snippets of life before then called up memories of the crib. I remember pulling myself up and peering over the bars at a long stairway down into oblivion. There were no toys in my crib, practically none in my life, except one: a ball. It was eight inches in diameter, a multi-colored striped ball. Mommy had written "Shari Kay" around the white stripe in blue pen ink. I treasured that toy for years.

It seemed as though I was always locked away somewhere. Mommy needed to punish me because I was obviously bad, although I could never figure out what I had done that was horrible enough to make her lock me in Daddy's old tool shed. Not even a pinhole of light penetrated the darkness. I sat stock still, huddled in a corner, afraid to move. I knew what was in there: tools, gas cans, yard implements, fishing poles and gunny sacks full of snapping turtles that Daddy trapped and stored there until it was time to kill and clean them. The darkness closed in on me. I was never quite sure whether or not the turtles would climb out of their bags and eat me. It seemed as though I was locked in there for an eternity. Even thirty minutes seems a lifetime to a three-year-old.

I was never warm. My little fringed buckskin jacket had no lining. Daddy had it made for me out of deer hides. Even though I liked to wear it, it wasn't enough to ward off the cold on those nights when Mommy and I walked the interminable three miles into town. To distract myself from the penetrating chill I played games with the oncoming headlights. I could see colors around bushes, trees, animals — even people. Mr. Peterson's apple orchard was particularly alive with color. I squinted my eyes and then opened them wide to make the colors dance.

Mommy and I walked up and down Main Street. Cars always pulled over and strange men exchanged a few words with her. The men never talked to me. Mommy put me in the back seat while she got in the front seat next to the strangers. I was always relieved to be riding in a warm car, even though we ended up in cemeteries, along dark country roads or deep in the woods. Sometimes Mommy moved me to the front seat while she and the man laid down and rustled around in the back seat. I slinked down, imagining that the dashboard was the control panel of a huge airplane flying me away. Sometimes Mommy locked me in the car while she and the man walked off into the darkness. I cowered on the floor of the car, sobbing, numbed by fear. What if Mommy never came back? Since these encounters happened several times a week, I soon learned not to bang on the window and scream. If I was a good girl, when the man took us back to town Mommy would call a taxi and we could ride all the way home in a warm car.

Sometimes policemen would stop and talk to Mommy. Then I got to ride in the back seat with Mommy to the police station. I liked that because the policemen always gave me a hamburger and a Coke. They must have known that I was cold and hungry. They gave Mommy and me a ride home every time too. It was a lot warmer than walking. One night, Daddy met Mommy and a policeman at the front door. The policeman stepped between them as they shouted at one another. Locked in the back seat of the police car, I was terrified by the loud voices, afraid that Mommy and Daddy would hurt each other, screaming, "I want my mommy! I want my mommy!"

I was so young I could never associate which particular behaviors of mine prompted Mommy's "spankings." They were totally unpredictable. She didn't require a reason. Her short temper flared into rage at the slightest provocation. All I knew was that if I made one false move, her long red fingernails reached out and sank into my arms. A blur of blows always followed. Beatings were random, vicious and unavoidable.

I must have been about four years old when Mommy sent me upstairs to the bedroom to fetch her a particular bottle of perfume. I couldn't read, so I had to guess which one among the two dozen bottles was the right one. I desperately hoped that I had chosen correctly. I brought the bottle down to where she stood at the kitchen sink and reached up to hand it to her. She screamed at me, "That's not the right one! That's not the one I sent you upstairs for! Can't you do anything right? What's wrong with you?" I prepared myself for the inevitable beating. She always picked up whatever implement was within reach to hit me with. This time it was a heavy wooden spoon. Her blows were relentless, first on the head, then the shoulders, then the torso. I screamed in pain, "No Mommy! No Mommy! No Mommy!" When the spoon snapped in two she continued to beat me with her fists. My body instinctively curled up on the floor into a protective, tight ball.

At that instant, like many such times before, I was lifted out of my body and I floated upwards towards an opalescent, pinkish field filled with hosts of angels. I glanced back at the tiny, cowering child on the floor, somehow secure that all was well. A pair of outstretched arms enfolded me into an overwhelming sense of well-being. I melted into its all-loving comfort. Then, suddenly, I found myself back in my body again as Mommy walked away from me. That's when I felt intense emotions of terror, pain and confusion. Sometimes Mommy was so nice and sometimes she was so mean. I could never make the connection about what tripped the switch to make her change moods. It didn't make any difference how quiet, how good, or how invisible I was: I could never escape. It was only a matter of time. It was only a matter of degree. If I couldn't avoid the beatings, I would just have to endure them.

Often I thought about the angels I visited while I was being beaten. I longed to be with them all of the time. I knew that wouldn't happen, but it was always comforting and peaceful to imagine them. My soft, detached floating feeling occurred again later in my life.

My only protection against my mother was her fear of my father. "Don't tell your Daddy ..." she admonished me. She was terrified that I might tell him that we were walking the streets at night while he was at the bar. She didn't want him to know that she was hurting me. I longed to be with him. Even if I never told him anything, maybe I could be safe with him.

Daddy was raised Amish and was by nature an outdoorsman. Every day after work as a carpenter he went fishing, hunting and trapping until dark. I was allowed to go hunting with him once. This was heaven for me, a singular moment, alone with my daddy, the only one I can remember. We walked deep into the woods together. When I realized that he was going to kill squirrels, I made a racket so that the squirrels would run away. After that, he sat me on a log and made me be quiet until he came back, squirrel tails hanging out of all the pockets of his brown hunting jacket.

My father must have been in his early thirties then. He worked hard every day and drank hard every night with his pals at the bar. Although he started drinking as a teenager, he drank even more now to escape having to care for two children — his wife and me. She was crazy — certifiably mentally ill, and I screamed through my early childhood. Daddy would come home at night and often find me dirty and hungry. One day I got sick and vomited all over the floor. He had to clean it up that night. He had no idea what to do about Mommy, about me, or about himself, so he avoided us. Even though he was unable to express his feelings, I knew that he loved me in his own way.

I bounced from one elementary school to another while Mommy took occasional part-time live-in baby-sitting jobs all over town. I hated school. It was just easier to be invisible, so I never asked for anything I wanted. Sometimes I would even pee my pants rather than ask to go to the bathroom. When Mommy worked for families in town, she walked me to school every day, almost as if she were concerned about what I might say to the other children. I felt isolated and withdrawn, afraid to speak or play. Even at home I was never allowed to play with the neighborhood children for long. Mommy's watchful eye made sure that I wasn't telling anyone what was happening to me. I never allowed myself to enjoy anything too much because I knew that soon enough I'd be called back. I learned to call myself back, even before I ever lived.

We lived out in the country next to a lake. A long, slim driveway stretched off from the main road to our house and to the neighbor's house twenty feet away. Ben, a huge, fat, beer-guzzling man and his wife Gert, a big woman in her own right, liked to gossip. They knew everyone's business in the neighborhood. That's why my mother never let me get too near them. That's why everyone in my life at that time seemed very distant. For six years Ben and Gert heard every word, every scream, every cry that came from our house. I somehow always felt like they were guardian angels. My mother used to hush me so the neighbors wouldn't hear. I didn't know then, but they were the ones who repeatedly called the police, "Come out here right now! There's a child being beaten." There were so many police reports filed on my mother, it soon became clear that she was unfit.

Of course, though I didn't anticipate it, Mommy was bound to get caught. It happened on a bright, sunny morning. Mommy had been out all night with a man at the cemetery while I slept on the back seat of the car. The man offered to give us a ride home, but needed to stop for gas. He pulled his big black car into the corner station and the attendant plugged the hose into the rear gas tank. I sat up tall so I could watch him out the back window. Just then, I noticed my father pull in right behind us and I exclaimed in sheer delight, "There's my Daddy!" I could tell by the frightened look on Mommy's face that this was not supposed to happen. Daddy walked over to Mommy's side of the car and said something to her. I could sense that she was surprised and that the game was over. Then he opened the back door and pulled me out of the car. I was eager to go with him.

I stayed at an aunt and uncle's house while Daddy worked and someone called a judge decided what to do with me. Everyone used a big word, "custody." Somehow that word meant something to do with my future. It was going to connect me with my next family. That word seemed to float through the air in whispers, "She doesn't have custody any more." "He doesn't have custody any more." It seemed that whoever got that word also got me.

My father's twin sister, Anna, got custody of me. Aunt Anna and Uncle Eli lived on Main Street in a tiny town in southern Michigan, population 600. Anna, Eli and their three-year-old daughter, Marie, were a typical Mennonite family. Aunt Anna always wore a dress covered with one of her printed aprons. She was meticulous. When she finished the supper dishes, she completely cleaned the stove, washed the countertop and swept the floor. She worked from dawn to dusk, driven by a poverty consciousness: work hard for your money and for your reward in the next world. She was a tall, comely woman, and sensible. "Waste not, want not" was her motto. Life was simple to her; she knew her place in it.

Uncle Eli, on the other hand, was more extravagant. He never seemed very comfortable. Maybe because he was shorter than Aunt Anna, or maybe because he lacked the appropriate seriousness about life. He seemed irresponsible and it made Aunt Anna feel insecure. He was interested in everything, even speed boats and electronics. He was certainly not typical of the family's stoic Mennonite tradition. He'd be positively giddy over his hobbies and playful with life, especially with Marie and me.

Marie was without doubt the most beautiful child I had ever seen. She had curly bobbing brown hair, and long eye lashes that I wanted to touch. Her large, warm brown eyes seemed to draw me in. She was a bit shy, but sweet, overly attached to her mother and sometimes whiny. Although I'm sure we fought, as children of three and six naturally do, I have no memory of it. She was such a delightful child. I loved her like a sister, feeling protective of her. I instinctively understood how precious childhood is, especially in contrast to my own.

Though the family always tried to include me in their lives, and treated me as though I was one of their own children, I could never be their Marie. Strangely, I was never jealous. Instead, I was in awe that she could play the part of a child so perfectly. And that her parents could play the part of loving parents so perfectly. I was such an appreciative audience. Somehow, I knew that this love would spill over on me. And it did. Oh how I loved them! I began to see what a real family could look like.

The whole family lived downstairs in a huge farm-style house. Marie slept in Aunt Anna and Uncle Eli's bed until they turned in. Then they would gently pick her up and move her to the couch, which they had transformed into her bed. There was no room for me downstairs so I slept in the guest room upstairs. I was all alone up there in what seemed like the deepest, darkest corner of the house.

At the top of the stairs was a huge bathroom that nobody ever used, except for the usual Saturday night bath before church on Sunday. It had an ominous, dark walk-in closet. I was so frightened by the immensity of the bathroom that I avoided it too, using instead the small one downstairs in Aunt Anna's bedroom.

My bedroom was furnished with two double beds and Aunt Anna's wooden armoire, with a long mirror in the front. The armoire was always locked. Although I knew that it held her special Sunday clothes, I also believed that there were boogie men in there. The same ones that were under the beds, outside the window, and in my big, spooky closet.

Aunt Anna and Uncle Eli left the hall light on when I went to bed. And I tried to race to sleep before they went to bed, because that's when they turned off the hall light. If they turned off the light before I went to sleep, I stayed awake for hours, terrified of the dark. Sometimes I screwed my courage up enough to walk out into the hall and turn the light back on. Then I would huddle alone at the top of the stairs, crying. That's when I remembered their whispers, *"Psss ... psss ... psss ... I saw her mother today in town ... psss ... psss ... She's still picking up men ... psss ... psss ... I heard she's having another baby."*

School was a wonderful experience, even though I was often the last to be chosen for the softball team. When I first came up to bat, I heard the other children's voices jeering at me, "She doesn't have a mommy or daddy so no one ever taught her how to play softball!" Even so, I always felt bigger and more competent than I could ever demonstrate. Maybe it's because I called on a higher power under my breath, "Just let me hit the ball." And miracle of miracles, I heard the bat crack and saw the ball sail into the outfield! The voices screamed differently now, "Yeah! Run, Shari, run!"

Because Aunt Anna and Uncle Eli were strict, practicing Mennonites, I was never allowed to wear pants. Two "everyday" dresses hung in the closet, one to wear after school one week, and the other to wear after school the next. I wore them to clean house, rake leaves, work in the garden and wash dishes. I owned three starched and pressed "school" dresses too, reserved for school and church only, one dress per week. There were two pairs of shoes on the closet floor, an everyday pair and a school pair. Every now and then I was lucky enough to get a pair of special Sunday school shoes.

Life for me was not perfect, but it was secure. I felt wanted. I vowed that I would make the best of this situation for as long as I had it. My life was balanced and predictable. I never wanted anything to change, except to go live with Dad.

Two years later, an angel was born. Baby David was the most precious infant I could imagine. He was fair-skinned and sensitive to everything, including lactose. His frailty demanded attention. In a Mennonite family it is customary for the oldest child to become responsible for all the younger ones. Since I was the oldest child, Marie and David became my charges, a responsibility that I never, not for one minute, resented. I held David constantly, bouncing him on my knee, and pulling him along, everywhere I went in my red Radio Flyer wagon.

Between my chores and watching over David, I still had time to spend with my few friends, like Nancy. Nancy lived on a big farm, with cows and pigs and a black and white draft horse named Sergeant. I spent as much time as I could with Nancy in the field setting up jumps made of boards and bales of straw. We played Annie Oakley for hours on end, timing ourselves to see how long we could ride bareback standing up.

I also was expected to help care for Grandma and Grandpa Yoder. Aunt Anna was always busy with David so she'd often send me on errands to her parent's farm. I'd look for excuses to ride across town on my green Western Flyer bike with the wire basket, handle bar streamers flying in the wind.

Grandma and Grandpa Yoder were pure Amish. They spent a lifetime on the farm, tilling it with workhorses and hand plows, and going to church in a horse-drawn buggy. They were upright, emotionally reserved people. Their lifestyle was a symbol of their closely-held religious beliefs, a simple, humble life within a bustling modern world. It was from them that I learned the spiritual significance of doing the commonplace with reverence.

Grandpa Yoder was a strong, sturdy man with a full, bushy beard, streaked with gray. He always wore a light blue shirt and dark blue pants, with suspenders and work boots. I remember him smiling and whistling while he worked, which was all the time. We went out into the fields and yelled, "Komboss!" The cows slowly trudged toward us for their evening milking. Grandpa sat on his milking stool, me between his knees learning to milk. I wrapped my little hands around the warm, swollen teats as he showed me how to tug and squeeze. He also taught me Pennsylvania Dutch words for "string bean," "flower" and "the Bible." I felt like a puppy, rollicking with him, tagging along behind him. I would have followed him anywhere. We would come in from the barn to the back room of a picture-perfect, immense white farmhouse and took off our rubber barn boots. He would lift me up to the water pump handle. I would push and push as water gushed out until the basin was full. We would scrub our hands and faces with Grandma's homemade lard soap, just in time for supper.

Grandma Yoder was a short, plump woman. She wore her streaked, gray hair twisted, wound up, and fastened to the middle of the back of her head, covered by a modest, white gauze cap. Round silver glasses accented the

shape of her face like a moon. And she smelled so clean —
the smell of *white*. She seemed ageless, although a life of
toil bowed her back a little, and she shuffled when she
walked, in modest, black orthopedic shoes.

Grandma always dressed in ankle-length, dark
dresses with a brown or dark blue apron pinned to her ample
chest. Solid round hips prepared her for making babies. She
had made five of them. And she made all of their clothes, including overalls and bonnets. There was nothing among the
domestic arts that she hadn't mastered: quilting, canning,
crocheting and gardening.

Grandma was a devout Amish woman who always
honored the Sabbath. That's why, after Sunday dinner, she
swept the already-spotless kitchen floor, scooped up
whatever dirt she found and dutifully put the dust pan and
broom behind the stove. Emptying it was the work. That
would have to wait until Monday.

Because there was no television in the house,
evenings at Grandma and Grandpa's were quiet and
predictable. Grandpa read farm magazines, and Grandma
mended clothes. Often we played jigsaw puzzles together. I
liked to root through the special box of toys they kept under
the stairway. Not "toys" per se, the box was full of wooden
spools and spoons, plastic molds, tin boxes, balls of yarn,
old lunch buckets, kitchen pails and genuine miniature John
Deere tractor replicas.

Soon it was time for dessert. With toys put away and
magazines folded, we went to the square oak table in the
dining room covered with a faded, stained, red-and-white
oilcloth. Grandma brought out bowls of store-bought ice
cream, always vanilla, always plain, and we talked about the
day's activities. My job was to take the empty bowls back
into the kitchen, then go in the bathroom to put on my

flannel pajamas. Then came the best part. Grandpa sat on my right side and Grandma sat on my left reading their Bibles, sometimes in English and sometimes in German. Spellbound, I sat silently between them in my pajamas listening intently.

Sometimes I asked Grandma to share with me what she was reading. She read to me in English and explained her interpretation of the verses. That's where I learned about God. She taught me the deep, devotional, all-encompassing love of God. I felt exalted by her spiritual piety, demonstrated every day by the genuine goodness she embodied.

Four of Grandpa and Grandma's children had become Mennonite, which allowed a little more worldly existence: electricity, a car, indoor plumbing, a telephone, buttons and zippers and a full high school education for their children. Since I lived with Aunt Anna and Uncle Eli, my life revolved around Sunday Mennonite services.

Up until now, I had never been exposed to religion, let alone the inside of a church. Attending church and hearing about an all-loving God gave me hope. Knowing that God really existed helped me make sense of my life. But sin worried me because my family said that I had come from a "sinful" home. The congregation treated me kindly although they seemed patronizing. Because they knew my mother and father — the drinking, the whoring, the child beating and the divorce — they looked down on me as a product of my parents' sinfulness. I felt like an outsider. I desperately wanted to be accepted unconditionally, to be truly one of them. But my past, over which I had no control, represented all that terrified them about worldliness.

That's why the story of the life of Jesus inspired me. I listened intently each Sunday about God's abiding love for me. I so gave myself to the experience that, just as I had gone to the arms of the angels when Mommy's beatings started, I went deep into the heart of God every Sunday. Enraptured, I overflowed with the power of God's love for me. For I knew that there, finally, I would be accepted unconditionally as His child. God had written me into his will. Grandma Yoder reinforced what I knew could be true for the children of God, because she lived a good life. And not just on Sundays, but every day.

Grandma grew the plumpest, juiciest strawberries I had ever tasted. During sunny summer mornings we'd squat over the dewy berries, picking one for the basket and one for me. Between morsels, I asked Grandma questions about her Amish life, "What is it like to live such a plain life?" "Do you ever want to go to a movie?" I was curious, constantly asking for clear descriptions and long answers to learn how she thought about things.

I asked her once about the visions of God and prophecy that Biblical characters saw. "Do you believe they really had them, Grandma?" She knelt silently for a moment as I continued to snap strawberries off their stems. I could see her face under her white bonnet, her eyes downcast. Then, in a low, prayerful voice, she began, "Well, Shari, I had a lot of questions, myself. And the biggest question of all was, 'Should I marry your Grandpa?' Marrying him meant that I would have to leave my church and join his. Was that what God wanted me to do? So I prayed and I prayed for an answer to that question, because I wanted to do the right thing. One day I was working in the garden, and the question was weighing heavily on my mind. Suddenly, I looked up from my work and saw a beautiful, bright white light. It was so big, it was all I could see. And I knew it was an angel. The angel said to me, 'Polly, marry this man and join his church. It is God's will.' So I did. And I know it was the right decision."

This story about an angelic vision from a person I loved and respected so much was undoubtedly true. She reassured me that if I were good enough, if I prayed hard enough then I could get help from angels too. I shared my story about angels with her, the only person on Earth who would understand it and accept me because of it, not in spite of it. She confirmed for me that other people, credible ones, had also seen angels. "Yes, Shari, angels are real. Visions are real. And there is far more to this earthly life than we can see." I rode on the wings of her words during all the years of healing my childhood wounds.

2

Going Back
To Daddy

My father did the unthinkable. He went into the Army during World War II. Amish are pacifists and therefore conscientious objectors. As much as Grandma and Grandpa wished the best for their children, they never judged them. When my father came back to the farm from the war, Grandpa scrambled down the road to greet him, wrapped his arms around him and cried tears of joy, "My Clarence is home!" Everyone knew that Dad was an alcoholic, in spite of heavy religious pressure never to touch a drop of liquor. All the while, Grandma and Grandpa simply said, "He has a disease." Divorce was absolutely unheard of among the Amish, but in view of the circumstances they felt that Dad had done the right thing by divorcing my mother, "It's too bad, but at least Shari is taken care of now."

In spite of it all, I was always told that I would go back and live with my father someday. For the entire seven years I lived with them, every Monday evening Dad came to visit me at Aunt Anna and Uncle Eli's. He proved how much he loved me by rarely missing a visit.

I prayed, hard, that he would get married again. That was the only way I would get to go back home with him. He had to provide a mother for me, and they both had to want me back. A year later, Dad met a woman named Beverly, who had a son, Ronnie, two years younger than I. In contrast to the Amish or Mennonite women I knew, Beverly was a "worldly" woman in her late twenties, with no religious background. She had light brown, short hair and a plain but pleasant face. Beverly was spunky; she didn't get bossed around by life. She had obviously been on her own taking care of Ronnie for a long time and was clear about what she wanted: a family environment and a nice home for her son. What she hadn't bargained for was Dad's preoccupation with drinking that only escalated over time, as did her temper.

Eventually Beverly and Dad got married. I was confused about why they didn't come for me that very afternoon, "It will take the court some time to award custody back to me. Try to be patient for a little while longer," he told me. There was that word, "custody" again. I was in a hurry. Going back to live with Dad would be my greatest dream come true. Instead, it turned out to be a nightmare.

During the next two years, Dad and his contract carpenters rebuilt the house he had lived in for years. I got in on the "ground floor," so to speak. Because I wasn't talented with power tools, or hand tools for that matter, my job was to cook for the crews. Dad designed a ranch style home with a daylight basement that opened out onto a lake. Beverly got a factory job to pay for brand-new furniture, since it was clear to her that my penny-pinching father would be content with tattered furniture forever. It was, indeed, the nicest home on our side of the lake. We all were proud of it. I felt lucky to get my own room. I chose to have it painted purple and selected floral curtains and a matching bedspread. Ronnie got his own room too, the small one next to mine.

By then I was in my mid-teens. My goals were simple: to fit in among my peers, go to all the school functions and swim in the lake with my friends every day. Instead, I found myself tip-toeing around Beverly each morning, never knowing what her mood would be. Generally it was bad. She was grumpy by nature, exacerbated by my father's drinking late into the night at the bars or the American Legion hall. Her bad moods usually meant that I couldn't be with my friends. Like Cinderella's, my chore list grew: clean the house, wash the dishes, set the table, cook the meals, tend the garden, scrub the floors, and can the beans — bushel baskets of them. Of course, there was no play until the work was done. Meanwhile, my stepbrother Ronnie's work was to take out the garbage and mow the lawn, once a week.

The household was spiritually void. I missed my Sunday religious experience at the Willow Grove Mennonite Church. Because I was not allowed to borrow the car, I made arrangements with generous congregants to drive me back and forth into town for church services. At the age when I questioned everything, I suppose it was inevitable: I sought a communion with God, not religious indoctrination or a narrow interpretation of Christianity based on strict dogma to which I had been exposed. I began to chafe at the restrictive Mennonite tradition.

It didn't make sense to me that if God were an all-loving deity, wouldn't all races and creeds be accepted into heaven? I had never felt damned in my life. Nor did I think that anyone else should, Christian or otherwise. More than that, I had too much history with the Mennonite church. Everyone there knew that I was the daughter of a "black-sheep" Amish alcoholic, divorced man and a whoring, abusive mother. I wanted a clean slate, a fresh start, somewhere that my background didn't matter. If my spiritual destiny was not to remain Mennonite, then what would it be?

Obviously, the logical way to choose a new church was to select the most exquisite architectural building. I looked for stained glass windows, huge, carved wooden doors, paintings, sculptures, padded pews, candles, flowers and an alter. These adornments stood in stark relief to the simple, white Mennonite church house with only wooden benches, a raised platform and a podium in front of a single, plain cross. I investigated all of the churches: Lutheran, Episcopalian, Church of Christ, Baptist, Church of the Nazarene. The Catholic experience with Latin, smoke, and holy water was exquisite, but it was also confusing. Do I stand? Sit? Kneel? What do the Latin words mean?

After architectural appreciation, the next level of awareness in "God shopping" was to find the church where the essence of religious teaching was alive in the congregation. If they lived and practiced what they preached, if they demonstrated spiritual congruence, they would no doubt accept me, for "Love thy neighbor as thyself" would be relevant in their lives. That place turned out to be the right hand side, second pew of the Wesleyan Methodist Church. The people there were warm and alive with "Godliness." It seemed that everyone wanted to be there. They experienced spirituality joyfully rather than dutifully. There were few "Thou shalt nots" and many "Thou shalts:" "Thou shalt sing;" "Thou shalt rejoice;" "Thou shalt love one another;" "Thou shalt share with one another;" "Thou shalt openly express all of it." I didn't have to sit in my pew quietly and piously. I could sing. I was finally liberated. The preacher and the congregation noticed my presence and even thanked me for coming. It became my Sunday home for the next two years.

All the while, Dad's drinking was getting worse. Beverly's volatile temper, coupled with her emotional neediness, contributed to the escalating noise level in the house. They bickered and argued constantly. It seemed especially loud in comparison with the serenity of Aunt Anna's. They bandied about another big word, "partiality." Dad and Beverly screamed back and forth, "You show partiality to your son!" and "You show partiality to your daughter!" Like any teenagers, Ronnie and I played off their power struggles. Ironically, however, we soon began to console each other by reminding one another that our parents' unhappiness needn't be ours and that we weren't to blame for their anger and pain. We soon forged a strong bond.

By now Beverly was unhappy all the time, and the mornings reflected it the most. If she noticed that the dishes or the ironing weren't done just so, I was grounded, "There will be no going outside after school, no swimming, and no dances for two weeks!" She never relented, and there was simply no way to be invisible around her. Her eyes were trained on me all the time. In the afternoons I could hear my friends shouting and squealing with laughter as they splashed in the lake while I dusted and swept. I was so infuriated I ran into my room, buried my head in my pillow and screamed at the top of my lungs, "I hate her! I hate her! I hate her!" Then I walked into the living room and smiled sweetly at her. I had to keep her happy if I was ever to have any happiness myself. It was the only hope I had to escape the perpetual grounding.

The situation seemed to intensify the more important high school became to me. School validated that I was
pretty and popular, so looking nice was a high priority.
Since I only had a handful of skirts and sweaters, I became
ingenious about expanding my limited wardrobe. For
instance, I borrowed clothes from a girlfriend and I learned
to sew so that I could make my own. I took baby-sitting jobs
that required me to live-in Monday through Friday. The
arrangement netted three bonuses: I earned money, I was
"legally" out of the house for a whole week, and my clients
offered me free reign in their closets.

Beverly had no taste and even less style. Bouffant
hairdos were the rage but she insisted that I pin my hair flat
to my head to keep my bangs out of my eyes. Even though
they were dated, I was forced to wear oxford shoes and
ankle socks, so I used my baby-sitting money to buy a pair
of fashionable tennis shoes. In the winter, when all the other
girls had shoe boots with fleece lining and matching
carrying cases, I had to wear brown rubber boots over my
oxfords, a double whammy. I enlisted a co-conspirator, the
bus driver, Bill. I hopped on the bus, made a mad dash to the
back seat, changed shoes, socks, boots and hairdo and
stashed my paper bag full of quick-change items behind his
seat in the front.

At the end of the day I changed back. The old school
bus ambled up our narrow road. I always sat on the left so I
could see the picture post-card view of the house and barn
on the hill kitty-corner from where our house was. There
were three bay horses, a pony and a burro in the rolling field
that stretched for forty acres inside a perfect white picket
fence. The bus squeaked to a stop, disrupting a horse-crazed
teenage girl's daydream. I picked up my stash bag behind
Bill's seat. He winked and smiled knowingly, "See ya'

tomorrow, Kid."

As the bus roared off, I walked over to the fence, like I did every day, in awe of the apparent wealth of the property owner. Although I'd never seen the man the neighbors called "Old Clyde," it was obvious that he never rode the horses, he just fussed with them. One day, from my fence station, I saw the silhouette of an old man leaning on a cane near the barn. He beckoned me up with a large waving motion. I looked around to make sure there was no one else he was inviting. It was me! I hopped down from the fence and scurried to the barn as fast as I could run. I was breathless with excitement and nervous about what he might want. Old Clyde seemed like a very fragile old man in his mid-seventies with red, watery eyes and thin white hair. He smelled of sweet pipe tobacco mixed with Old Spice after shave. My eyes fixed on the goiter next to his Adam's apple. He looked tired, but there was an odd steadiness about him. I expected him to say, "Stay off that fence young lady!" Instead, he looked at me, his watery, brown eyes gleaming like hot coals and said in a strong clear voice, "I'm having this mare, Lady, trained for riding. And I'll need someone to keep up her training, a regular rider." He pointed his pipe, wrapped in stubby fingers at me, "Do you know how to ride?"

I was quite confident that I was a capable rider, after all I was Annie Oakley. "Sure!" I would have said anything to climb on the back of that magnificent horse. I had never seen anything like her. Farm horses were usually chunky and scruffy with tails full of burrs. Lady was a Standardbred, a sleek trotter. Her shiny coat glowed almost burgundy and her perfectly-configured slim legs, with long black stockings, clip-clopped along, barely clearing the ground. Equine fashion at the time preferred a "Mohawk" mane and cropped tail. Not for Lady. Her flowing black mane and tail, combed and perfectly trimmed, snapped in the wind like silk Crusader flags.

She possessed a regal bearing, reflecting the same sophistication of Old Clyde's picturesque horse farm. I'd never felt regal in my life until I sat on her back. I was sophisticated by association. I carried it with me forever. I knew that when I was finally in control of my adult life, I would choose to surround myself with the beauty I had appreciated so many afternoons sitting on Old Clyde's fence.

Lady was smart and sensitive, both to my commands and to my emotions. She could sense when I needed a slow, graceful, quiet ride, like a rocking chair. On other days, when I felt wild, we cantered lickety-split through the fields. Lady never tried to buck or brush me off under trees. She never shied. She so trusted my riding skills that she went anywhere I asked her to go, even into the lake.

We often rode to the swimming hole at the far side of the lake when I was sure no one else was there. Lady raced along through the water's edge, splashing and kicking up fans of sand and water. I took her saddle off and walked her deeper and deeper into the cool, green lake. At knee level, she pawed the water, splashing it all over me. Finally, when it was too deep for her to walk any further, she began to swim. I slid off her back and swam freely beside her. We glided through the cool water for about ten minutes. Then I let her graze on tufts of shore grass until she dried enough to be re-saddled.

From that point on I became Lady's companion and Old Clyde's friend. Lady became my lifeline. I daydreamed about her during school. I couldn't wait to get home, to finish dusting the hardwood floors, or prepare for the evening meal so I could scoot up to the barn. I practiced, in vain, being invisible so that Beverly couldn't see me and assign me another job. On weekends, I headed for the barn after morning chores and didn't come home until dark.

Old Clyde transformed me. He refined my rough, self-taught skills and channeled my raw enthusiasm into a capable rider. I learned how to sit on a horse properly, to give knee commands, to ride both Western and English style. He'd say "Leave your troubles behind now and go for a nice ride." Sometimes Old Clyde followed us in his shiny, black El Camino. With his elbow propped over the open window, he watched us gallop down Gray Lake Road at top speed, billowing dust behind us.

Other times we just sat together, Old Clyde propped on his dented, red tractor seat, welded to a pipe stuck in the ground, while I sat at his feet, patiently combing out burrs from Red, his Irish Setter, with the curry-comb from the barn. Old Clyde asked me, "What do you want to be, Shari?" Strangely, no one had ever asked me that before. But I knew the answer. It was clear. "I want to teach mentally retarded children." I'd known that ever since I baby-sat for Tommy, a 13-year-old profoundly retarded boy who was destined to spend his whole life in a crib.

He encouraged me. "Don't believe what your stepmother says about you, that you're worthless and will grow up to be just like your mother. It's not true. You can do anything you want to. Don't be limited by anyone else's limitations. The *sky's* the limit for you. Remember that."

My relationship with Clyde became the most important influence in my life. He had been a total stranger and loved me for no reason at all. And I loved him. He was like a father, guiding me, directing me, caring what happened to me. He never expressed his affection in words, but he demonstrated it in obvious ways.

For instance, teenage girls from around the neighborhood soon began to sniff around after they saw me riding through the fields on a beautiful mare. Melanie, from the next lake over, was horning in on Lady. One day, late in the afternoon, Melanie took Lady on a long ride, groomed her, and put her away for the night. When I went up to the barn at 5:00 as always, I couldn't help but notice that there had been an interloper in my relationship with Lady.

When Clyde discovered my broken heart, I turned away from him, making quick swipes at my tear-filled eyes. "I know that Lady is your horse," I said, "and I don't have a claim on her, but I just so wanted her to be *my* horse. I love her as if she were my own, that's all."

His eyes watered even more than usual, "Shari, you don't ever have to worry about that again. Lady is your horse."

I sobbed even louder, awed by the fact that he loved me so much to give me his horse. He had no obligation to me. More importantly, I had done nothing to earn such a love. "Really? Oh, thank you! Thank you!" I threw my arms around his neck and kissed him on the cheek, careful to wipe off any trace of tears I had left there.

My confidence soared. Old Clyde had given me two great gifts of a lifetime, a horse of my own and a new identity as a worthy human being. I practiced worthiness at school as well. It was completely different from the identity I had at home. The same smile I forced for Beverly, became genuine at school. Oddly, I was voted "the happiest senior." Underneath it all, I still felt so inadequate and inferior that I didn't dare try to join a clique. Instead, I worked the crowd in the cafeteria, going from table to table smiling and greeting everyone. I focused my energy on studying, even though my grades, as usual, were average.

With Old Clyde's encouragement, I tried to help my father and stepmother understand that I fully intended to go to college. The big question, of course, was how I would fund my schooling. Beverly would not let Dad give me any financial support for college unless he gave an equal amount to Ronnie. "If you do for her, you have to do for him." Since Ronnie was clearly not college-bound, Dad refused to give him money for any reason. That meant I was in financial trouble.

I marched up to the barn. This setback deserved a long ride on Lady. Afterwards, Old Clyde was waiting for me on his tractor seat, smoking his pipe. He said, "You know, you can always borrow money to go to school."

"From whom? I don't have the grades for scholarships."

"If you go down to Citizen's State Bank and tell them that you want a loan to go to college and tell them that I sent you, I bet you'll get some help."

I did exactly what he told me to do and got a $3,000 loan on the spot. It wasn't until twenty years later that I realized Old Clyde greased the skids to my college education, both by encouraging me to follow my dreams and by giving me the financial resources to help them come true.

3

Off To College

None of my father's Amish generation ever went beyond an eighth grade education. Plying a trade was more practical. As their children migrated toward the more liberal Mennonite tradition, educational horizons expanded. In certain circumstances, higher education might be considered for the eldest boy. Women, of course, had their rightful place on the farm. There were sixteen grandchildren on the Yoder side of the family; none of them had gone to college. I was swimming upstream against familial and religious heritage. There was no precedent for me, or for my family, to support my decision. Nothing in their background, mentality and experience could help my family understand why someone, especially a girl, would want to go to college. I knew why, although I couldn't say so out loud. The practical reason was that I could become a teacher and support myself. The real reason was that college meant freedom, pure and simple. I chose Eastern Michigan University, in Ypsilanti, two hours from home, because it had an intimate feel and a strong Special Education department.

It was fall, 1967. The hippie movement was in full swing, offering the format for self-exploration. I loved school. I loved studying. I loved expanding intellectually. Bell-bottomed and beaded, I now got to choose when I came in, how to spend my money, even when to do my laundry. Despite its opportunity for unbridled recklessness, I managed to balance academic achievement, average as usual, and personal freedom.

A college course launched me on another spiritual journey. I found myself, a wet-behind-the-ears first-semester freshman, sitting in an upper division Philosophy of Religion class. On the first day, a tweedy, eccentric professor entered the small circle of ten students and announced, "This is Philosophy of Religion, 301. My name is Dr. Adams. In front of you is your syllabus. We'll be meeting here on Monday, Wednesday and Friday at 10 a.m." He paused while everyone glanced through the three-page syllabus. As they focused back on him, Dr. Adams flatly stated, "There is no God." Then he left the room.

I was stunned. I cried for days. I went to Emma, the dorm mother, in tears, "What kind of place is this? I think I should go home." I stayed on despite the challenge to all my beliefs, and I began to sort through the pieces of my spiritual foundation, carefully evaluating what was true for me. I believed in an all-loving God, who lived outside of me. I envisioned my God more like a force than a being. I talked with this force in my own form of prayer. It never occurred to me that a prayer was a request that could be denied. I simply declared what I needed in the moment and felt guaranteed that I would be assisted with it, one way or another. Still unable to swallow the notion of one true religion, this class showed me many spiritual paths and inspired me to explore my own definition of "God."

Patsy was flamboyant, a large girl who loved to wear scarves and hats and beads together. Her thick brown hair swung in her face as she spoke animatedly about seeing things like "energy fields" and perceiving different kinds of "spirits" like the wispy form who rocked in the rocking chair in her tiny apartment. Although she was comfortable about sharing her life with disembodied spirits, her stories made me very uncomfortable. They seemed spooky and somehow different from my own profound angelic experiences.

These two explorations, college coursework and Patsy's perspectives, prompted me to consider alternative ways of perceiving the physical and mysterious aspects of life. By examining the meaning of my small world, I found that I could extrapolate my experiences into a bigger one. I was in my element, consciously designing and participating in my own life. I began to pay attention to the magnificent coincidences in it.

I experimented with "spirituality" and learned about psychic phenomena from Patsy. She helped me discover that I had psychic abilities because I could accurately describe details in her life that I had no conscious way of explaining.

But an event in the summer of my sophomore year diverted me from mystical investigation. And the coincidence of it changed my life forever. I was back at home with Dad, Beverly and Ronnie to earn money for the next year of college. Dad loaned me his old, beater station wagon to drive to work at Bailey's Restaurant/Truck Stop/Motel right off the Indiana toll road. I pulled the all-night shift, waitressing from 10 p.m. to 7 a.m. Then I changed out of my greasy-smelling polyester "waitress whites" into old jeans to clean its sixteen motel rooms until 1:00 in the afternoon.

After work, I went home, changed in to my swimming suit, tucked my pillow under my arm and fell asleep out on the dock, near the lake, in the sun. There was still time to take a spin on Lady occasionally, and to see my friends. Life seemed perfect and predictable. I was in charge. And in three weeks, I'd return to the excitement of school again.

Woodstock weekend was coming up. That Thursday night, several friends asked me to go with them to the music festival. But I couldn't justify giving up a week's worth of wages and tips on a frivolous junket. Reluctantly, I decided not to go.

By Friday midnight, I had worked up quite a pity party for myself. All my friends were at Woodstock while I stayed behind to wait on tables. Since the restaurant was empty, I wasn't earning any tips anyway. Just then the glass door squeaked open and through it walked a six foot three, tall, dark, slender hitchhiker who had just gotten off the toll road. His figure filled the doorway. He wore black bell-bottoms, a black long-sleeved tee shirt, a wide leather belt and a string of turquoise beads around his neck. He had shoulder-length dark brown curly hair and piercing brown eyes. He was the most handsome man I had ever seen! I was so nervous, I tripped over my own feet to wait on him. My face was flushed and pasted into a smile. I was unable to speak.

Darren simply ordered coffee. Then he explained that he had been hitchhiking on the toll road to Woodstock. I muttered a few words about not being able to go, and he quipped, "You don't look so busy now. You can go with me." When I explained why I couldn't go to Woodstock, he stayed and talked with me for a few hours. At 4 a.m., he decided to get a room in the motel out back. "Wake me up when you finish cleaning rooms." He left a five dollar tip.

We were magnetized to one another. I couldn't wait until my shift was over. "Oh my God, what if he's gone?" "Oh my God, what if he's *here?*" "Why is he interested in *me?*" "Who is this guy anyway?" "What do I do with him?" "How do I explain him to my parents?" "How do I explain him to *me?*" I couldn't seem to train the butterflies in my stomach to fly in formation.

I discovered that weekend that Darren's father was a prominent surgeon at Johns Hopkins University. Darren enjoyed a privileged life. He could afford the experiences that made him charismatic. He had traveled extensively around the United States and was comfortable in many social scenes. He could speak convincingly about any subject. He had overcome a drug addiction at one point in his past, and had even been married for a few months.

How could someone so worldly be attracted to me? Darren made me feel special. He even gave me his turquoise necklace. Our passion escalated to such a feverish pitch that we soon decided we had to be together. Since Darren was less committed to his living arrangement and to completing his studies than I, he agreed to move to Michigan to be with me. We rented a small yellow cottage with a charming arched doorway and a spacious back yard a short distance from the campus. While I attended classes, Darren took odd jobs as a window decorator for local department stores.

Had I been paying attention, there were clear signs that trouble was brewing. For example, an old boyfriend of mine, Stewart, who had remained a friend, dropped by the house to visit. After he left, Darren threw a jealous fit, accusing me of seeing Stewart secretly, and of caring more about an old boyfriend than about him. Nothing I said could calm him. The more I tried to assuage his anger the more agitated he became. He shouted obscenities and raged, "I'm leaving!" Defiantly, he raided all the money I had in my wallet and stormed out the door.

Having never seen his temper, I was confused, lonely and frightened. I broke down, sobbing uncontrollably. I didn't know what to expect. Bits of memories flashed. When Mommy raged, the beatings always followed. Would he have hit me? He didn't know anyone in town. Where would he go? Back to Maryland? Would he calm down and come back?

After a few hours, Darren reappeared, drunk. He apologized, barely. "I just got carried away. If you hadn't talked to Stewart, I wouldn't have lost my head." My response, ingrained after years of subconscious practice, was to try to make the situation right. It was obviously my fault. How could I convince him that I loved only him? Darren wanted to make love. But after such a terrifying emotional upheaval, sex was the last thing on my mind. I gently pushed him away, reminding him that he had been drinking, "Can't we talk for a while? I'm really confused about what happened tonight."

He flew into a rage again, pulled me toward him and hissed through gritted teeth, "You'll make love *now*. And you'll *like* it." My survival instincts kicked in. I went limp and acquiesced. Unlike Mommy's rages, I was unable leave my body this time. No angels carried me away. I simply endured his violation. After Darren had satisfied himself and fell asleep, I lay beside him, crying silently, bewildered by love's illusion shattered.

The next morning Darren turned toward me, blinked sleepily, and smiled that tender smile that he knew would soften my heart. He reached over, stroked my hair and whispered softly, "Hi, Sweetie." I melted. Darren was back; the sweet, gentle, handsome man I loved was here again. His expression evened as he propped himself up on one elbow, "Shari, I want you to know that I'm so sorry about last night. I love you so much, I just went crazy. I promise, it'll never happen again. Never!"

With every ounce of power at my command, I willed it to be true. The thought of life without this handsome, charismatic man was unthinkable.

I refused to worry about it again. Life returned to normal. I started each day at 8:30, working in the on-campus school for handicapped children and attending upper division Special Education courses in the afternoon. Darren got a full-time display job at the local J.C. Penney store.

Of course, almost inevitably, I became pregnant. The baby, which we agreed to name Christian if it were either a boy or a girl, would cement our love forever.

The hardest thing I had to do was to tell my parents. I knew they would be outraged. I expected a shrill, "I told you so" from Beverly so I avoided making the phone call as long as I could. Several weeks later, I forced myself to make the call. "Hi, Beverly. I've got some news. I'll get right to the point … I'm pregnant."

There was a long pause at the other end. In her usual snippy voice, Beverly said, "Well you know what that means, …"

I thought, "Here it comes, her moment of glory. She's been waiting a long time to gloat."

"First off, we have to tell your father. Then we have to start getting you the things you need for that baby."

Stunned by her response, I stuttered, "Oh … uh … okay…. Well, I have nothing … so that's a good place to start."

"I understand what you're going through, Shari. I understand how confusing and scary this can be. I went through something like this myself, and I didn't have anyone to help me. You see, Ronnie was born when I was a teenager."

Our relationship changed from that moment on. My condition would give her the opportunity to offer help when none had been offered to her. My baby would provide a child in her life to take up the space that Ronnie left when he graduated from high school and moved away. She needed to be needed and I was in no position to reject her help. I took her up on her offer to break the news to Dad.

Meanwhile, the relationship between Darren and me steadily worsened. Darren drank more often now. He was a mean drunk, saying cruel things to me like, "If it weren't for me, you'd have to go home to your mom and dad." It was useless to argue with him during these episodes. I made excuses for his behavior; he was obviously nervous about the added responsibility of becoming a father. He would soften up, surely, when the baby came.

To prepare for our marriage, we took the required blood tests. But the day before the wedding, something inside me balked. I was getting married because I had to, because it was socially acceptable. It would appease my family. It would satisfy all the conditions. But it wasn't out of choice. I suggested to Darren that we postpone the wedding until after the baby came.

"No sweat!" To Darren, the important thing was that we were making a family, the legal details were insignificant. To me, getting married was such a "forever" commitment that I couldn't consign myself to it until I was sure, really sure, that everything was perfect.

And it was. Over the next months I refurbished a crib and prepared the nursery. My friends hosted parties and showered me with baby supplies. Almost daily Darren came home with a new toy for the baby. He rubbed my stomach and felt the baby kick. In those days it was unusual to see a college student wearing long Indian madras dresses with a pregnant belly underneath. I wore my blonde hair long and straight and parted in the middle to reveal gold-rimmed wire granny glasses. I was a flower child, round with new life, completing junior year finals.

Two goals were in sight: only one more year of school and only three more weeks until the baby arrived. The weather was hot and humid. My toes were beginning to look like Vienna sausages. I waddled when I walked, as pregnant women do, so I minimized activity. It was difficult to keep up with Fergus, a small short-haired terrier that Patsy left with me to care for while she was visiting her parents in Boston for a week. Fergus was used to being a lap dog, and I didn't have much lap left.

Darren and I were invited to a Fourth of July party. This was a perfect opportunity for him to drink to the birth of his baby. Our friends clapped him on the back with "Congratulations, Daddy!" Darren was the life of the party, generously helping himself to the beer keg all day long and well into the night. As he weaved his way to the car heading for home, I knew I'd have my hands full. I resorted to my usual "Don't rock the boat" behavior to avoid his drunken meanness.

When we opened the door to the cottage, Fergus was delighted to see us. He spun around with glee and jumped up on us. Darren closed the door quickly so that Fergus wouldn't run out into the street. It was then that he noticed the scratches in the wood. Fergus had been pawing so vigor-

ously to get outside that the plywood door had deep stria-
tions in it. It would have to be repaired.

One glimpse at that, and Darren snapped. His mood
changed in a heartbeat. He yelled, "You little bastard!" and
started hitting the dog as hard as he could. Confused and
helpless, Fergus tried to run away. Darren snatched him up
and hurled him across the room. The dog hit the wall, hard,
like a bird against a window, and slumped to the floor. I
thought he was dead.

I was frozen in panic. I silently went over to Fergus,
careful not to utter a sound, and scooped him up. He
cowered, stunned by the fury of what had just happened. I
carried Fergus into the nursery and closed the door to get as
much visual and physical distance as we could from Darren.
I sat in the rocking chair, stroking the trembling dog, tears
streaming down my face. I knew that it was only a matter of
time before that rage would be unleashed again, this time on
me or my baby.

I waited in the nursery a little while until Darren
passed out in the bedroom watching television, like he
always did after drinking too much. I felt sick to my
stomach and weak in the knees. I couldn't understand how
I could love such a kind and gentle sober man and loathe
such a raging despotic drunken one, at the same time.

I carried the dog out into the living room and laid
down on the sofa with Fergus nestled against me. Relieved
that Patsy was coming home tomorrow, I cried myself to
sleep. In a few hours, I awoke in excruciating pain. I knew
it was only gas pains although I couldn't relieve myself. The
pain escalated into agony. Concerned that this might cause
a problem for the pregnancy, I called the hospital. The nurse
reassured me sweetly, "Well, Honey, you're in labor. So you
better get here now!" This was obviously a misdiagnosis,

the baby wasn't due for another three weeks.

I was reluctant to wake Darren, unsure of his response or of his ability to help me. But I had no choice. I jostled him. "The hospital says I'm in labor. We have to go right away." Thankfully, he had slept off enough of his drunk to function. He drove the twenty minutes to the hospital, delighted that his baby was about to be born, "This is it, Honey!"

He clearly didn't remember a thing. I sat in numbed silence, eyes straight ahead, "Yep, guess so." I felt no excitement about the baby coming, after all it was only gas pains. My mind toggled back and forth between the pain in my body and the pain in my heart.

Darren screeched up to the emergency door at St. Joseph's Hospital. A Dr. Kennedy was waiting for me in the examination room. She placed a sheet over the lower half of my body while she checked the baby's position, "You're dilated four centimeters. It's definitely labor pains you're feeling. And everything looks fine." In an instant, I focused on my baby. Whatever had happened before this moment dissolved into a dim memory.

Christian was coming.

4

The Wake-Up Call

"Christian" was born a perfect baby girl. Although she was three weeks early, she emerged with a full crop of brown hair and dark eyes, like her dad. I stared at her, an infant flawless in every feature, for hours on end. I would see to it that her life was not like mine. She would be given a normal, happy childhood.

Darren was captivated by her as well. To him, she represented his most perfect creation. She seemed to fill some kind of emptiness in him. His tenderness returned. He picked up the sleeping child, his big hands enfolding her, and whispered, "You're so beautiful!"

Friends, most of whom did not have children, lavishly doted on Christian and on us, the perfect couple. Darren loved the limelight. Because of the spell the baby cast on all of us, I remained hopeful that life would continue just like this, forever. But I wore blinders. With my senior year delayed because of our shaky finances, I had to face up to our rotting relationship. Darren's drinking escalated. He went to a friend's house nearly every night for four or five hours and came home stinking drunk, and mean. One night, frustrated because his dinner was cold, he shoved his plate across the table and snarled, "Can't you do any better than this shit?" He jerked my hair around his fist. I tightened my neck, unsure of his next move. Out of the corner of my eye I saw him sweep the catsup bottle off the table. He shook its entire contents over my head. Catsup oozed over my ears and down my neck. He shoved me away from him, and in a humiliating finale, he laughed, "There! That's what you deserve."

I had suffered his indignities and forced sex for a year and a half. So far, I had eluded any real physical harm with the exception of the occasional shove or slam against the wall. All, of course, accompanied by a dehumanizing tirade of curses and name-callings.

Throughout my life, my typical response to Mommy's unprovoked beatings, Beverly's arbitrary moods, and Darren's mercurial rage was to go silent. Silence was required to try to find the center of myself when I felt confused, panicked, angry or resentful. Thus, the only choice I seemed to have when Darren went crazy was to be silent, sulky and distant. I was trapped. Also, I had a baby to consider.

Darren was particularly short-tempered when I didn't read his mind, or respond to his clipped order-barking, especially when we worked on the car. On one of the first warm days in late spring, while I played with Christian in her playpen out in the yard, Darren insisted that I help him by handing him the tools he had spread out over the lawn. Stooped over the sputtering engine, he snapped, "Get me the wrench!" As I tried to determine which of the five he meant, the order shot back, louder this time, "The big wrench, stupid!"

Scanning the possibilities, I panicked, my welfare was at stake. My mind raced, trying to make the right decision: "Is this one the big one? Is it the biggest one? Are these the wrenches? Oh my God, which wrench does he want?"

"Where is it? Can't you do anything right, you dumb bitch?" By this time, Darren had stood up and impatiently walked over to me as I knelt on all fours furiously comparing wrenches. With his hands clenched together in a single fist in front of him, he raised it up over his head and brought it down in the middle of my back with the full force of his strength.

A reverberating pain shot through my body and I collapsed. I couldn't breathe. I couldn't even gasp. I thought, "I'm hurt. And I'm going to die. So I might as well let you know that you really did it this time." I refused to pass out, to lose ultimate control. Rather than remaining silent in my pain, this time I dared to express it. I had one chance to make this drama hit the mark. I exaggerated, coughing deeply and writhing in pain, moaning and gasping loudly. I let my eyes roll back, struggling to sit up.

Darren was stunned. He bent down on one knee and stared at me. He reached over, took hold of my shoulder and shook me lightly. "Shari, Shari, are you all right?"

I did it! I had his attention. He was scared. This was the split second that I had control. I needed to know that I could control the danger, even for an instant. But once Darren saw that I would be all right, he stood up and walked back to the garage, muttering, "Next time, just give me the damn wrench when I ask for it."

For the first time I admitted to myself, "There has to be more than this in life. This isn't how it's supposed to be.

This isn't the kind of life I want for Christian. And if I can't get it for myself, how can I possibly get it for her?" For once I didn't retreat into the whirling fog of confusion. I could think and I could think clearly. This episode wasn't my fault. There was nothing I could have done to avert it. It was a set-up, one that I'd lose either way. I remembered all the other set-ups from him and from Mommy. Just because it felt familiar didn't mean living this way was my only option. Even though I owned nothing, and felt like I was nothing, I knew, in the depth of my bones, that there had to be more to life than being someone's punching bag. I made a feeble, trite promise to myself, buying time to figure it out. "If he ever does it again, I'm leaving. And I'm leaving for good!" even though I didn't have a clue how.

I spent every day with Christian, focused on being the best mother I could be. I researched the phases of developmental learning, devising appropriate games for her skill level. I read books to her. We played together for hours every day. She was balancing herself on furniture and getting into everything. I even made a game of finding creative ways of rearranging the house so that I didn't have to say "no" to her all the time. I delighted in watching her grow and develop. In one week it would be her first birthday.

Darren stayed away from home more frequently now. No doubt he could sense my disillusionment about him, but he could always count on being in the spotlight with our friends. Since he brought the beer he was always welcomed. Darren usually came home late, around eleven o'clock. I avoided drunken confrontations with him by laying in bed, feigning sleep. Weekends, however, he drank all day, which meant he'd be cocky and bullying when he finally appeared at home. One particular Saturday night, it was shortly after eight. Curled up on the sofa, watching television, I cringed when I heard the back door slam.

Darren made a pass through the kitchen, pouring himself a tall glass of milk and grabbing a handful of homemade chocolate chip cookies from the jar. He sat down beside me on the sofa, grunting a muffled, "Don't you have anything better to do than sit around watching TV?" When he came home this belligerent, I braced myself for a potential explosion. He shoved a cookie in his mouth, turned to me, and said matter-of-factly, "Like to have sex?"

Something snapped. I wasn't about to oblige him in any way. Suddenly, I heard my own voice challenge him, "I wouldn't make any kind of love with someone like you if my life depended on it!" In that second, I realized that I couldn't pull the words back into my mouth. And I knew that his hair-trigger rage would make me regret I ever spoke them out loud.

I was wearing a plain white short sleeved tee shirt and a pair of blue jeans. He grabbed my sleeve and yanked me towards him. He jeered, "We'll see about that!" and threw the glass of milk in my face. I pushed against him with all the strength I could muster. While holding both wrists with one massive hand, he slapped me across the face with the other. Tearing at my clothes, he tried to force himself on me. I scratched his forearms, wriggled out of his grip and lunged away from him.

He shoved his foot between my ankles and I toppled to the floor. He began to kick me, relentlessly. The thuds landed on my head, between my shoulders, deep into my buttocks and along my thighs. All I could think was, "I have to get away! I've got to escape." Adrenaline kicked in and I managed to scramble away far enough to get my legs back under me.

I instinctively ran toward the back door; so did he. He snagged the belt loop on the back of my jeans. As I lunged hard for the door handle the belt loop snapped and I was free. I bolted into the back yard scanning the neighbors' houses for a light. None. I turned and ran into the street. Passing cars would surely deter him.

I felt his hands clutch my shoulders as he spun me around. Frenzy flashed in his dark eyes. How dare I countermand his order? He would make me pay, and pay dearly for my insubordination. He shoved me against a car, the door handle dug into the small of my back. He put his hands around my neck and gripped hard. His long, powerful thumbs pressed in on my trachea. Somehow, I found reserves enough to push against him. Instinctively, the more I thrust my arms into his chest, the harder his thumbs dug into my throat. He was choking the life out of me.

In a split instant, I realized that this was it. This time Darren really was going to kill me. All of a sudden, I remembered Christian. She was still inside the house, sleeping. Somehow, I knew that I had to live. I wasn't going to give over to him, or anyone else, the right to take my life or my baby. I would do whatever it took to live. I tried both survival modes, fight and flight, neither worked.

I did next what I knew best how to do, I let my body go limp. I closed my eyes, my arms dropped to my side, my knees buckled. I let my body fall against him. Darren loosened his grip. He stepped forward to prop me up. When I sensed that he relaxed a bit, I drew in a few labored breaths, enough to whisper hoarsely, "I'm so sorry ... I'm so sorry ... It's all my fault. Let's go back into the house."

I wiped the blood off my face and dragged my fingers through my milk-soaked hair. I let Darren lead me back inside. I made it a point to behave as usual, quiet, distant, dutifully picking up the mess in the living room. The routine couldn't be disturbed, not now, not while I was planning my escape. I filled three bottles for Christian, as I did every night. But this night, I made mental notes. Meanwhile, Darren laid down on the sofa to watch TV and polish off the cookies he'd left on the table. Relaxed from alcohol, exercise and venting his anger, I heard him begin to snore lightly.

This was my chance. It was the only chance I had. Like a mouse, I tiptoed into Christian's room, picked up the diaper bag on top of her changing table and stuffed a handful of diapers in it. I pulled her crib blanket around her, and gently lifted her out of bed, careful not to wake her. Ever-so-quietly we edged back through the living room making sure that Darren was still passed out. The even heaving of his chest signaled his deep sleep. It was close to eleven. I went to the kitchen, retrieved the three bottles of milk from the refrigerator, and shoved them into the bag. Christian and I slipped through the back door.

Once outside, I ran as fast as I could to the end of the street, turned right, and ran the four blocks to my friend Joanne's house. Christian began to fuss. My legs burned. My lungs felt like they would explode. Thank God! Her light was on. I pounded on the door furiously. As she turned the handle, I pushed my way in, gasping, "I need help! I'm in trouble! I need to catch my breath for a minute, while I figure out what to do."

Joanne's eyes were as big as saucers. She took Christian from my arms. "Of course, Shari." She offered me a chair next to the fireplace. "Sit down and rest a while. You're safe here." I panicked when I realized that I was on the run with a baby and a diaper bag, and nothing more. The most logical thing to do was to call Dad and Beverly.

When Beverly answered the phone, I broke down, sobbing hysterically. I had no idea what to do or even how she could help me. She stopped me in mid-sentence with a staccato command: "Stay right where you are! I'm getting in the car right now. I'll be there in two hours." Those two hours seemed an eternity. Darren also knew Joanne. It would be safe here only as long as he was passed out. I had no jacket, no purse, and no money. I tucked Christian in a makeshift bed on the sofa and paced like a caged animal, whispering, "Hurry, Beverly, hurry."

When Beverly pulled up to the curb, Christian and I jumped into the front seat. I pulled the bulging diaper bag in beside me and slammed the door. "Quick! We've got to get out of here! Darren might know where I am."

Beverly had it all planned, "We're not going anywhere except to the police station. Darren has no right to keep all your personal effects. You need things for the baby and the police will help us get them." I was so thankful for her.

Three policemen escorted us to the house while I collected my purse, my clothing and all Christian's baby supplies. I felt safe. I could claim what was mine, including my personal sovereignty. Sensing my new liberation, Darren began to sing his siren's song, "I didn't mean to hurt you, you know that. We have a wonderful thing going. We promised to build a life together, you and me. What about our beautiful baby? How can you take her away from me? How can you take care of her all by yourself?"

Even in the heady flurry of packing to escape, I stopped for a moment to listen to him. Beverly stayed at my side, picking up everything that she could find for the baby and me. She watched me soften, ever so slightly, and snapped, "Get back to packing your baby's things, *now!*"

Her familiar voice jolted me into reality. Of course! Christian was the most important thing in my life. She had inspired me to live. I brushed the crusty blood from my forehead and smiled wryly to myself. It really worked! I played dead to have a chance at life. And this time, nothing would stop me.

5

Have Diaper Bag Will Travel

In those first few weeks after I left Darren I was a listless zombie. All I could do was sleep and cry. I should have felt safe,. Instead I felt numb, lonely, afraid and empty. Traumatized by the thought that the man I once loved had tried to kill me, I dared not admit that I still loved him. But I was truly in love with the *idea* of him: a big, strong, handsome, intelligent savior. This tender stranger swept me off my feet. I wanted the fairy tale. I wanted to be taken care of and live happily ever after. But this tale ended with Darren's fingers wrapped around my throat. I grieved not about losing him but about losing the fairy tale. Like many women, I was addicted to the fantasy.

Dad and Beverly allowed me to wallow in the stupor of my depression and fog for three weeks. On the stickiest evening of the summer, we sat around the kitchen table after dinner, wishing the door, propped wide open, would breathe some relief. Dad angled his elbow across the table at me, leaned into it and asked, "Well, what are you going to do now?"

I couldn't answer him. I absently shrugged my shoulders in silent blankness.

Beverly wouldn't accept that answer, "Stop thinking just about yourself and start remembering that you've got a baby to take care of. You can only stay here for so long, so you'd better be coming up with a plan."

Forced to face reality, I began to inventory my assets. I had a beautiful child, three years of college under my belt, food and shelter, and I knew how to get and keep jobs. Because I had nothing left to lose I suggested the impossible, "Do you suppose that you could give me a loan to finish school? I'd minimize the cost by staying with friends for a couple of months, so I'll only need money for books and tuition."

My father agreed to loan me money, interest free, and with no specified payment period. But every time I requested something out of the ordinary, that is, other than books or tuition, he evaluated it with heavy sighs and hesitation. Each amount was always noted in a small, blue, spiral-end notebook. For instance, he helped me buy an old red Nash Rambler that caught our eye as we drove by Chevy dealer. We road tested it, kicked the tires and looked under the hood. Dad bought it for $500.00 and jotted the amount in the notebook.

I appreciated his help. It was the only hope I had. And it was a very small price to pay to get my life back in control. His generosity would eventually earn him another dividend, the personal satisfaction that his daughter needed his help to get through school, and that he was able to provide it.

Beverly volunteered to be responsible for Christian's care while I went back to school, and proved to be a very affectionate grandmother. She took Christian to a photographer for a portrait sitting and accepted nice hand-me-downs from her friends. She even hired Marjorie, a tall, lanky 60-year old who answered the ad for a nanny.

From September through December I slept in the corner of a friend's living room. I rolled out my sleeping bag at night and shoved it into the hall closet during the day. I earned my space on the floor by cleaning up the kitchen and scrubbing the bathrooms. When I could, I left $20 to contribute to the electric bill, but the floor remained cold and hard. By Christmas, I was ready for a change. As much as I appreciated my friend's generosity and friendship, my values had shifted. Sleeping on the floor, eyeball to dust ball was no longer appropriate. I was a mother responsible for a baby girl. And my student teaching courses meant preparing lesson plans each night. How would my students respond to a teacher who had to sleep on the floor of someone else's home? There had to be a better way. I had been "putting up with" and "making do" all my life. I deserved more.

I called my long-time friend, Peter, who like me, had been living with his parents in another city, saving money to come back to school for spring semester. He suggested that we get a house together and find another roommate to split the rent three ways. I appealed to my father, once again, explaining that my living situation was getting in the way of my schoolwork. I was carrying a full academic load so I couldn't hold a job to cover the additional $125 monthly expense. He agreed to loan me the additional money each month and carefully noted it in his blue notebook.

From an ad in the student newspaper, Peter and I found our third roommate, Janey. We lived in an old, but clean, house, with our own rooms. I reclaimed my privacy by taking the upstairs bedroom. I drove to Dad and Beverly's every weekend to visit Christian. It was Thursday and my stomach ached. This week I had no money left over to buy gas for the drive. I couldn't imagine a weekend without her.

I resorted to prayer, as I always did in times of desperation, "Please, God, help me find a way to get gas money so that I can see Christian." I walked across the quad toward my next class, breathing deeply to relieve the tightness in my stomach. I became aware of a piece of paper stuck to my shoe. A miracle! A five dollar bill! That one tiny coincidence brought back a powerful childhood memory. God was always present in my life, but I had been so busy surviving, I couldn't recognize the constant small miracles at work here. I was in awe of this mystical coincidence. What would have happened if I prayed for a ten dollar bill?

I raced home the next day to see my baby. She was radiant. It was clear that she was thriving under Beverly's care. At eighteen months, she changed daily, speaking new words and mastering new skills. Although Christian was always excited to see me, it took us at least a full day to re-establish our relationship. It was difficult for her to have me come and go. I suffered with separation anxiety all weekend, dreading five o'clock on Sunday night. I tried to minimize our anguish by hugging her, saying matter-of-factly, "Mommy will see you again in five days," and scooting out when she wasn't looking. Nothing worked. No matter what we did, neither of us could avoid crying. Christian followed me to the door, sobbing, "I want my mommy!" I drove at least 45 minutes of the two hours back to school through a veil of tears.

Eventually, I faced the fact that I needed Christian with me and acted on the suggestion of Janey, our roommate, to apply to an agency called "Aid to Dependent

Children." I went to the office, completed the forms, and discussed my situation with a case worker. Because Christian's father had disappeared and I was a full-time student in the student-teaching program I seemed an excellent investment. ADC gave me financial assistance for food, rent and medical insurance for Christian. What's more, they offered me money for in-home child care. And Janey volunteered to look after her part time.

Christian became the fourth person in our apartment. She infused a whole new energy into our college scene: high chair, play pen, crib, Dr. Seuss books, toy chest, dollies, and childproof gate at the top of the stairs. She was an inquisitive toddler, constantly chattering, whose huge brown eyes and sweet smile melted everyone's hearts. She made her wishes clearly known, like insisting that whoever was sitting on the sofa read her favorite book. Christian changed all of our lives during those six months.

That June I completed my student teaching, bachelor's degree and job interviews. Starting in the fall, I would begin my new career as a Special Education teacher in rural southern Michigan. I did it! I reached my goals without compromising my vision. The diploma and teaching certificate were tickets to a new life, a life that I would create for Christian and me. I thanked God. I knew that the trials I had gone through must have a purpose in my divine plan.

6

Facing
My Fears

Beginning my professional career flushed up all the fears I had ever faced. First of all, I had never lived alone. Secondly, I was afraid of the dark. Thirdly, I was afraid that terrible things would happen to me like getting raped, physically injured or even killed. But those fears were small potatoes compared to the big one. I was afraid of what other people would think of me.

Yes, I had credentials. Yes, I interviewed well. But what if I wasn't a good teacher? What if they saw who I really was? Me in charge of fifteen profoundly retarded children? They obviously had mistakenly placed their confidence in a sniveling, quaking little girl. There was no evidence that I could travel in the world, literally or figuratively. After all, I had allowed myself to be a physical and emotional shut-in for the year and a half I spent with Darren. I was so crippled by self-doubt that there were moments when I even questioned my ability to be a good mother. Literally, I was afraid of my own shadow.

I set about to find a place to live that would help me stand up to the ghosts of fear. I realized that they were only specters, neither justified nor real, but they ran my life. I would feel safer in a neighborhood or an apartment with someone above, below and beside me. If I chose to live the country I would, indeed, be all by myself. Contradicting my own logic, I decided that since I was going to be alone anyway, now was as good a time as any to start picking off my personal demons. I began looking for a house in the country.

I found a cavernous, two-story farmhouse with dark corners, an echoing attic, and a dank, musty barn. It stood alone on a lonely country road. I knew that there were spooks alive in that house. I actually considered renting it, then came to my senses and gave myself permission to develop bravery at a more reasonable pace.

Instead, I chose an 800 square-foot, cracker-box cottage guarded by an ancient billowing willow tree. It was plain, white, and single-storied, with no frills, not even a porch. There were few nooks and crannies for me to keep track of and two doors, one in the back and one in the front for quick exits.

Even though it was eight miles out of town at the end of a dead-end road, there were three other houses along the way, close enough that I could run to them in an emergency. The cottage faced Fox Lake, a small, gray-blue fishing lake that froze over in the winter so that Christian and I could ice skate. The lake buzzed with life in the summer with swimmers, frogs and wild ducks.

The cottage was perfect for Christian and me. It came furnished with a stove and refrigerator, an overstuffed, scratchy green sofa with long fringe along the bottom, and a faux marble Formica table with chrome legs and four chairs covered in matching gray Naugahyde. Christian and I even had our own bedrooms.

My room, as usual, was simple. An old, scratched dresser left behind by the previous tenants called for a floral dresser scarf that I made from a piece of fabric picked up from a garage sale. The hand-me-down double bed from Dad and Beverly's house was covered with a handsome gray velour bedspread, an ingenious transformation of an old stage curtain from the college Drama department. I cut around all the scorched parts and hemmed it to fit perfectly. I covered the top of a small wooden bed stand with a lace doily and an old oil lamp I found at a swap meet. The comforting smell of kerosene reminded me of Grandma's house. I needed all the comfort I could get out there, all alone, at the end of the road, in the dark.

Christian's bedroom was a showcase. It represented the hope that she would have love, security and stimulation, all the possibilities of a full childhood that I could dream for her. She was two years old, ready for a "grown up" bed, a twin-size found in the local classifieds. She inherited my old oak dresser from Dad and Beverly's house that blended into the blond paneling. Beverly sent along a yellow bedspread and even more children's books. Next to the bookshelf I placed Christian's small pink tea table with wrought iron legs and two little pink padded chairs. Dad had given this set to me years ago when I lived with Aunt Anna and Uncle Eli. Christian's toy chest, painted with balloons and clowns, bulged with stuffed animals, dolls and developmental toys.

I got a red Irish setter, Strider, for companionship and protection. He weighed seventy-five pounds and had a deep, threatening bark. I felt safe during the day, but I tensed up at dusk, feeling anxious about the inevitable darkness. In the country there are no street lights and no business signs, just pitch-black darkness, the kind that miners know a mile under the earth. Some nights were worse than others. Even though everything was locked, I braced chairs in front of both doors. I lay in bed for hours with my eyes jammed shut, praying that sleep would overtake me.

On the bad nights I had a routine. Chairs bracing the doors, I literally checked every corner: peeked in the closets, looked behind the shower curtain one more time, and peered under the beds. The darkness was alive and palpable. I could feel blackness lurking inches from my face like an ominous hot pillow. I fended off panic attacks through sheer will power. In every room I kept the lights on and the interior doors open all night long. Sometimes this routine carried me through a week or two of quasi-restful sleep. Often, I sat straight up from a sound slumber, convinced that I had heard a noise. I lay there, frozen, straining to hear it again, even though Strider slept motionless. Every morning I said a prayer of gratitude, "Thank God! I made it through another night."

I spent two months cowering in nightly terror. I told myself that what I feared didn't exist anymore, that it came from being locked in the car in the cemetery at night; it came from being randomly beaten; it came from almost having the life choked out of me. No matter how I rationalized, fear gripped my nights. I was afraid of the darkness of my own soul. I knew that if I conquered this phobia I was on the way to recovery.

I began to overcome my fear of the dark by turning off the light in one room and leaving the others illuminated all night. It took weeks for me to turn off all the lights in the house. I started with the light in my bedroom. There was still enough light streaming in from the living room to see. Next, I turned off the kitchen overhead light because it was around the corner and I wouldn't miss it anyway. Then I switched off the light over the kitchen table. The bathroom light was a critical juncture. If I awoke and had to go to the bathroom, that light allowed me to see clearly all the way. The overhead light in the living room just contributed to the general luminosity, it wasn't really necessary. I got down to the last lamp, next to the sofa, the one that projected light into my dark bedroom. It took weeks before I dared to think about turning it off.

One night I finally felt unusually courageous and turned off the sofa lamp. I slept only a few minutes that night. The next night, I left it on. Then off. On. Off. On. Off. It didn't mean that I wasn't still afraid of the dark. I remained terrified every single night of my life. The only difference was that the fear wasn't crippling me anymore. I could function, inconsistently at first, in spite of the fear.

A month passed as my confidence edged back even though I still twinged at the thought of sleeping in total darkness. One night, I awoke to the sound of something rustling in the brush outside my window! I could hear it moving around the house, swishing through the leaves.

I lay like a corpse for a solid hour until I was sure that whatever, or whoever it was, it wasn't coming back. I slowly pulled my arm from under the covers, reached over and flicked on the lamp. I slid out of bed and raced from room to room, flipping on all the light switches. I sat on the sofa, huddled in my grandmother's quilt, thinking "Why am I so afraid? Is there really something out there? Oh, my God, is it Darren?" I cat-napped until the sun came up at 6:30 the next morning.

In the clarity of daylight, I realized that the sound I

heard was probably a raccoon. I wasn't in any real danger last night. It was clear that I was afraid of something that wasn't even real. It was finally time to overcome fear of the dark once and for all.

I tackled the problem, using the same process, all over again. I flicked the lights off, one by one, in the same order, over a period of several weeks. Eventually I got down to the pure darkness of the country again. Amazingly, I actually began to sleep. I finally conquered the darkness! The memories remained, but they no longer ran my life. Since then, I have been able to sleep in any dark house. But every now and then, if I had an uncomfortable, insecure night, I still gave myself permission to leave a light on.

My job at the Hillside County School was to teach all ages of trainable retarded children from infants to age 25. I soon discovered that all my academic assignments in theoretical education classes, and even as a student teacher, were, to say the least, irrelevant.

I took one look at the children streaming into my classroom and gasped. Fifteen children showed up, ages 6 through 17. Some came in wheel chairs, some burst through the door, some wandered aimlessly around the school until either my teacher's aide or I retrieved them. They had totally diverse needs and each required a unique, specialized, individual training program. From Sarah to Billy, they required the full range of attention. My carefully-crafted academic lesson plans were useless. Sarah, age 15 and diapered, lived in her wheel chair. It was difficult to determine if she had any social skills, but she could somewhat communicate her needs even though she was spastic and had extremely limited verbal capability. She was very stimulated by the other children. Sometimes she would laugh and emit joyful noises. Because she was placid, it was easy to wheel her into position, lock the wheels and forget that she was there. My challenge was to remember that Sarah, and other quiet children like her, deserved my attention as much as the demanding ones like Billy.

Billy was hyperactive, darting uncontrollably around the room, demanding attention, picking up and dropping one toy after another, scribbling on the walls and constantly chattering. I learned what would help him calm down: a highly structured environment, calm and even speaking tones, and holding him on my lap. That was a problem. Billy was eight, and the son of a retarded woman who didn't understand how to care for his physical requirements. He peed his pants every night and came to school in the same clothes the next morning. He reeked of urine, so it was unpleasant to get near him, let alone put him on my lap. Soon Billy's schedule included a warm morning bath in the tub that the school provided for helping these students learn independent living skills. He also got a clean change of hand-me-down clothes from the teacher's aide's son.

Once again, my life offered me the opportunity to drink from a fire hose. My one-room schoolhouse represented the gamut of age, physical needs, as well as developmental and social skills. I was overwhelmed. It was clear that I would have to start at square one. Goals and objectives were required for each child, so I got a crash course in teaching, social work and all kinds of therapy: physical, speech, occupational, art and music, not to mention parent-teacher liaison, and even cook.

In a matter of a few weeks, I managed to integrate chaos and diversity into a smooth-running classroom that met each child's needs and was fun for the staff. The same structure I created for the classroom, I was consciously and simultaneously creating in my own life. At home I became aware that all the lights were turned off at night and I felt safe and secure. I was happier. Since I wasn't used to having money, and certainly wasn't used to spending it except on necessities, for the first time cash accumulated in my savings account.

After the school year, I rewarded myself by giving in to the urge to travel to Alaska. Because I didn't want to make such a long trip alone, I invited my former college roommate, Janey, to be my traveling companion. In mid-June we headed north. For two months we drove across Canada, through the Yukon Territories and up into Alaska. I could taste adventure. People along the way were awed that we made the trip alone, two single women with a two-year-old child. Since we had planned so carefully, the risk seemed minimal. We took it for granted.

Alaska is the land of the midnight sun. Throughout the summer a mystical twilight hung in the night air. We hiked up to a magnificent incandescent turquoise glacier, an almost unnaturally brilliant color. In the stillness of the crisp mountain air, we could literally hear the glacier, moaning and groaning its way though the valley.

We watched gray whales in the Pacific, learned how to dig for clams and took a canoe trip down the Moose River. As we canoed I lost myself in a sense of oneness with nature, paddling in tune with the river's flow. Along the banks, sometimes curious moose followed our silent silver canoe. When we portaged overland, carrying the canoe on top of our heads, along with our heavy camping gear, I found strength in my body that I never knew I had. By the fifth portage, I lifted the canoe as though it were only a bushel basket of cabbages.

Exploring Alaska was an expansive experience, and I expanded with it. I had planned and executed a beautiful adventure! By the time I returned home, I was brimming with self-confidence. I finally knew, within every cell of my being, that I was powerful in creating my own life. I also knew something else. My awareness was expanding into a deep appreciation of the mystical by experiencing the magnificence of the physical world.

7
Professional / Personal Growth

Armed with moxie after the Alaska experience, I was more willing to try new things with my students. Their special needs demanded innovation. Most Special Education departments were organized around isolated classrooms of specified age groups. I initiated a building expansion at the school and set up study areas focused instead on skill mastery. A workshop equipped with tools helped students learn pre-vocational skills. In the arts and crafts room students developed their creative abilities. The language arts room taught them to remember their names and addresses and learn to write them if they could. We even built a mock-up of a studio apartment with a bed, sofa, TV, conventional bathroom and washer and dryer to teach the students basic life skills, including personal hygiene. They learned to count and to value money. Just like their mainstream counterparts, our students moved from one room to another during the day which gave them more stimulation, helped them learn to follow directions and safely get from one place to another. The entire focus of this innovation was to help students become as independent as possible. Today, of course, it's standard to find these features in Special Education programs.

I was contacted by the regional director of Special Olympics to participate in their program which offered athletic competition to all ages of the mentally retarded. Competitions were held twice a year locally, regionally and state-wide throughout the nation. Spring events featured track and field and swimming, and winter events featured skiing and skating. Athletic achievement and competition gave these students the opportunity to express another part of their personalities. It didn't make any difference if the children came in first or last, they just competed as best they could and received as much praise and applause as the winner.

My aides and I trained our students for Special Olympic events as part of their regular physical education curriculum. Not only did they learn physical skills, they also learned the rules of the game, how to stay in their lanes and how to be a good sport, like not hitting the person who wins the race. We encouraged them just to do their best, no matter what. Everyone participated. No one was excluded.

Our kids met others like themselves from surrounding schools and began to socialize with them. I could see their sense of achievement and their pure delight just to participate. They loved being there. It made them feel good about themselves. Michael, a 14-year-old Down's syndrome boy won the silver medal in the 50-yard dash wearing big brown work boots. A broad smile lit up his face as he ran around to all the participants and coaches showing off his medal. He grabbed my hand and pumped it in wild congratulations (sometimes they were confused about who was to be congratulated), "Mith Thewi, Mith Thewi, Look! Look!" Even those students who didn't win a medal won a participation award. Everyone got to bask in the glory that they had been someplace special and done something important.

Our school district kicked in as much funding as possible to support the program. I approached local service clubs for donations and project support and enlisted community volunteers to launch fund raising events such as 10K runs and rummage sales. Special Education majors at the college volunteered to help the children learn to throw a softball. Retirees volunteered to chaperone the participants during competitions. Soon the program expanded to 75 participants, including the educable mentally retarded from Special Education classes in mainstream schools throughout the county.

For the first time in my life I was very visible. I became accustomed to being in the foreground, the focal point. My picture appeared in the local newspaper virtually every week. Colleagues teased me constantly, clipping out my picture and taping it to my mailbox with the caption, "Your name in lights *again?*" I quickly moved from county coordinator for Special Olympics to regional director for three counties. I was passionate about the program and its benefits to my students. I organized and hosted regional events and coordinated hundreds of children, volunteers and teachers. I began to notice that when I spoke about Special Olympics, something came over me. It was more than enthusiasm. Words flew out of my mouth as if I were not in charge of them. Some part of me seemingly moved aside and another part of me took over. I lost all track of time and place. Audiences were spellbound by my intensity. At the end of each talk, I seemed to click back into consciousness to answer their questions.

I noticed another thing. Although I really loved teaching children, there was something I loved even more, teaching teachers and managing programs. My skills and talents could be more influential and I could make a bigger impact from an administrative perspective. I began to set new professional goals for myself.

Under the guise of professional development, my Special Education district covered 50 percent of my tuition to pursue a Master's Degree in Special Education Administration at Eastern Michigan University, an hour and a half away. I took night classes while Christian stayed at home with a baby sitter. I studied after she went to sleep at night and every weekend. Once again, I thrived in the academic setting. This time I carried a four point average almost all the way through graduate school because the coursework was stimulating and directly relevant to my career. Three years later I received my Master's Degree.

Meanwhile, I administered innovative programs, supervised four aides, taught students in the classroom, and ran the Special Olympics program. I eagerly assumed all of the responsibilities of a school administrator. Finally, I asked my superintendent to acknowledge my increasing scope of responsibility by changing my title to "Program Administrator."

At the next board meeting the title change was granted. It was the ticket to making important contacts at state-wide conferences for school administrators in Special Education. In effect, it launched my administrative career. I met Dr. Morgan, the director of all specialized programs in an adjacent county. One year later, he invited me to interview for an administrative position. Although it was a rare opportunity, I evaluated his offer carefully because I was perfectly happy where I was. But my span of influence could increase exponentially in this new position. I took the job, nearly doubling my salary.

It was now possible to consider buying my own home, even though I was a single mother.

The property I found was a two-story, four-bedroom white farmhouse with cedar shake siding, under three giant maple trees. It had a small front porch and a wrap-around back porch. Its five acres supported a duck pond and a run-down chicken house, with enough room left over to put in a garden, a pasture, and eventually a barn. The property was completely surrounded by cornfields and woods. On the other side of the gravel road were soy bean fields. Although the farm wasn't nearly as quaint and picturesque as some of the others I had seen, somehow I knew that it was mine. A gentle breeze always whispered across the property, so I named it "Breezy Five Farm."

The century-old house sported high ceilings and pristine oak trim throughout. But that was all that was pristine. There were no closets anywhere and virtually no electrical outlets. But I could see its tremendous potential. It required a lot of work and elbow grease, but I willingly signed up for the job.

It had a typical country kitchen, an expanse of floor space and no cupboard space. The tiny counter top next to the single, chipped porcelain sink was covered in bowed, cracked linoleum. Green wallpaper sprinkled with tiny orange flowers had long ago given up sticking to the walls. The newest items in the whole house were an avocado green stove and refrigerator. Dirt ground a path across the yellowed speckled linoleum flooring into the dining room whose arched doorway hinted at beautiful double doors that must have been installed there at some point in its life.

My bedroom, to the left of the dining room, had a plain wood plank floor. The walls were covered in faded yellow flowered paper. I lifted up a chunk of it to reveal four layers of successively ugly paper beneath. Its almost floor length windows were bare. Christian's room was the tiniest in the house. But a fresh coat of paint on its plaster walls and a new carpet made it immediately livable for her.

There was an unusual room in the center of the home, probably originally used as a living room. We converted it into a sun room by furnishing it with wicker furniture and big potted plants that drank in the sunlight from southern windows.

Upstairs there were two bedrooms, one was a long narrow, but potentially comfortable room with windows on two sides. But its plaster walls were cracked and the ceiling was falling in. The grandest bedroom, across the hall, had floor-to-ceiling windows on two sides that framed the vista of farms and silos forever.

I was looking forward to transforming this spacious and solid house. Its foundation was firm and its support beams were neither cracked or insect-infested. And the updated heating, electrical and plumbing systems were in good shape.

Soon after I moved in, my college roommate, Peter, came to visit. He had planned a two-week vacation from life in Colorado, looking for a change of scenery. Attracted to the rhythms of farm life, he soon got a job with a local house painter and never left. He moved into the big upstairs bedroom and offered to help me transform the property.

I acquired two horses. Sunray, a bay mare, was given to me by her owner who could no longer afford to keep her. She was gentle, responsive and obedient. I could put anyone on her back, assured that they would have a safe ride. As a papered thoroughbred, she would make a perfect brood mare. I received a phone call from a friend who said, "I think you should come over and take a look at this horse my neighbor wants to sell." Azakiah was 16 hands high, a gray registered Anglo Arab gelding with a white tale and white mane. I took him for a ride in his pasture. Accustomed to a gentle but crisp ride, I was thrilled by Azakiah's powerful rocking-horse gallop. He was a perfect contrast to Sunray's gentle nature.

Azakiah and Sunray would be fine in the pasture through the summer. But it was clear that we needed to raise a barn to protect them from the harsh winter soon to come. Peter and I laid the cinder blocks for a 30 by 60-foot pole barn. But the barn poles, sections and trusses needed to be assembled by a professional. So I called my father who was by now the superintendent of a construction company, and asked if he would supervise a small army of friends that had volunteered. Over the course of the next few months, Dad came over on weekends and helped us erect the structure. Although he teased me about going through so much trouble for dumb horses, Dad made sure that the building was well-built and sturdy. He was sober during the work process, but rewarded his progress afterward with beer after beer. That's when he'd refer to the project as "that Goddamned horse barn."

I had mixed emotions about his help. As usual, there was a string attached. On the one hand he seemed genuinely glad to help raise the barn, and on the other he couldn't resist making comments about its foolishness. One Saturday evening after work on the barn was complete, Dad went inside the house to get a cold beer and came outside to sit next to me on the back porch, "You know, Shari, I've been thinking about the money you owe me, you know, that college loan."

"Oh yes, I've been thinking about that too. I can start paying it back now. Let's come up with a monthly amount."

He interrupted me, "No. I'd rather just drop the whole thing."

I was dumbfounded, "But why? I must owe you at least $3,000 dollars!"

"It's $3,472.60 to be exact. But I don't want you to pay back any of it. I don't need the money and besides that, I was glad to be able to help you with your education. You wouldn't have been able to finish otherwise, I know."

His generosity touched me. Dad had no intention of ever collecting on the loan, but his pride didn't allow him to give openly and unconditionally. He needed to give on his own terms, even though they felt like strings to me. At that moment, I chose to see them as requirements of his generosity not as impediments to my accepting it. I leaned over to him and put my arms around his neck, "Thanks for helping me, Dad."

While the barn was being built, I scoured farm and estate auctions looking for an Amish buggy, a holdover from my memories of handling the reins, while Grandpa's big hands behind mine gently guided his horse. The one I eventually found wasn't Amish, nor was it a buggy. Rather, it was a large open "Abraham Lincoln" carriage with wrought iron steps, two full black upholstered seats, a black leather trunk, and the original wooden wheels. As nearly as I could figure it was made in the late 1800s. The carriage was too massive to fit in the barn, so we transformed the old chicken house, about the size of a two-car garage, into the carriage house.

I lived near several Amish communities where it was quite likely that I could find an excellent trainer for Azakiah and me. I asked around town and two names kept coming up, "Jake and Johnny" Bontrager. At first they were reticent since Amish people only train other Amish people's horses. When I explained my heritage and told them my last name, they recalled having heard of my grandparents. So Azakiah went to their farm, twenty miles away, for three months while he trained to pull the carriage. Since Jake and Johnny worked with Azakiah after their chorin,' I was able to get lessons twice a week after work and on weekends. Grandpa sent me an article from the Amish newspaper, "The Budget," a newsworthy item about Jake and Johnny training Azakiah, "a horse owned by the granddaughter of an Amish family." I had become like kin to them.

One summer evening I met up with Jake and Johnny by the back door of their farmhouse. Their older brother, Samuel, in his thirties, was paralyzed from the waist down and confined to a wheel chair. He watched his brothers from behind the screen door in the kitchen as they hitched up Azakiah to their black buggy and put him through his paces around the yard. Jake and Johnny clucked at Azakiah, "Gittup! Gittup!" At that moment, I heard a singular angelic voice rise above their sharp commands and Azakiah's hoof beats. Samuel's strong, yet delicate tenor sang out simple devotional hymns. His voice instantly transported me back to childhood days when I left my body and went to the bosom of the angels. It quickened the memory of all that I held sacred. I was moved to tears.

Another Amish man, Elden, a jack-of-all-trades, agreed to take a look at my antique carriage. He had a white flowing beard that blended with his shoulder-length hair, not unusual for a man in his seventies. He was an enigma. A convert to the Amish faith at age 28, he remained warm and open, collecting pen pals from all over the world. I secretly hoped that my name would stay on his list. Elden hitched up his horse, Ruby, and took the carriage for a test run. He greased and repaired the shafts, wheels, and all the mechanical components and even reupholstered the seats in shiny black leather. I was confident that the carriage was next to new.

When Azakiah's training was complete, I brought him home to his own pasture. Since the Amish neither own nor drive cars, the following Saturday I picked up Jake, Johnny, and Samuel and stopped by to get Elden as well and brought them to my farm. This was an important day for all of us. Samuel watched from the car while Jake and Johnny helped me harness Azakiah. Elden wheeled the carriage from the carriage house and hitched it up to Azakiah's harness.

I clambered up into the driver's seat and insisted that Jake and Johnny come with me. Jake hoisted himself up and sat to my left while Johnny positioned himself in the center back seat. They sat up tall, anticipating the maiden voyage. I snapped the new leather reins and chirped, "Gittup!" Azakiah's ears flicked. The carriage creaked then lurched forward, metal wheels shushing through the loose gravel. I heard the familiar clip-clop-clip-clop, as the immense carriage jangled effortlessly along the road. Azakiah trotted proudly in front of the smartly refurbished carriage. One snap of the reins instantly conjoined our activities of the last few months into the consummate unity in this moment: horse, driver and carriage merged into a perfect Currier and Ives scene. This carriage represented all the cherished aspects of my childhood. I drank in the joy and awesome-ness of it all.

I was profoundly moved by the realization that all of my dreams had, indeed, come true. I had claimed my rightful place in the universe. Anything I had deeply wanted had actually materialized. I owned a beautiful farm that nurtured my soul. My small family unit was well-adjusted and happy. And my professional achievements aligned perfectly with my talents and interests. All aspects of life were fulfilling and stimulating. I finally accepted the tangible evidence that I could experience joy — joy of my own making. I didn't have to deserve it, earn it or allow it to be beaten out of me.

I sat erect, hypersensitive, silently guiding Azakiah down the road alongside the farm. Suddenly, I glanced to the right and caught a glimpse of myself standing at the side of the road studying the carriage as it rattled by. Oddly, I was in two places at the same time, bi-located, both within the scene and appreciating it from a distance. From my vantage point by the side of the road, watching myself drive by in the carriage, I was overcome by a sense that there was something bigger than myself, a divine plan, operating through me.

I understood that I was drawn to desire this life because it was clearly in line with my soul's higher purpose. That's why I could manifest all that I had desired as effortlessly as Azakiah pulling the carriage. All my experiences had prepared me for this realization, the fulfillment of lifelong dreams that my Spirit wanted for me. Momentum was in my favor toward an even more promising future. I was one with it for that instant in time.

8

Sally

The following October, I attended an educational seminar that introduced innovative behavior modification techniques for severely retarded students. A teacher from a nearby county approached me during the lunch break, to ask for further clarification on a point I had made earlier. She glanced at my name tag that read, "Shari Yoder" and inquired, "Oh, by the way, do you know a Sally Yoder?"

My mind flashed. There was only one Sally Yoder that I had ever heard of. It was murmured in low voices at Aunt Anna's and whispered among the neighbors around Dad and Beverly's. I gathered from these rumors that my biological mother had a second child whose name was Sally. "Yes, I've heard of a Sally Yoder, but she couldn't be the one you're referring to. Why do you ask?"

"Because we have a Sally Yoder in our severely mentally impaired classroom. And the name is so unusual that I thought you might be related. Right now we're in the process of collecting enough evidence of child abuse to remove Sally from her home."

I went into a tailspin. I felt sick to my stomach. My mind ping-ponged: "Could it be true? No, it can't be! I know it's her. No, it couldn't possibly be her. If it is, I know exactly what she's going through. Child abuse? Retarded? Oh my God!" I knew that this unfortunate girl was my half-sister but I resisted taking the emotional ride of my life. "What's her mother's name?"

The voice came back, "Edith Yoder."

Her name seared into my brain like a hot poker. Stunned, I stood motionless for a few seconds, then regained a modest composure, "Yes ... I guess that would make Sally my half sister. I've had no communication with her mother for twenty three years. I had no idea that she had a retarded child. All I knew was that she gave birth to a daughter named Sally nearly eighteen years ago."

The rest of the seminar was a blank. For the next few days I was consumed by thoughts of having a half-sister. This was not a strange child living in India. She had come down the same birth canal that I did. It was impossible to brush off. "Why was I saved? Why couldn't she be saved too? I had guardian angels who came to my rescue at a very early age. Why didn't she?" I couldn't resolve the paradox.

I knew exactly what her life was like. If the school was just now trying to remove her, Sally must have endured horrible random beatings for eighteen years! I cried at the thought of what she was going through. I cried for her pain and for my guilt. I felt guilty for being whole, for being happy, and for having a good life when I knew that hers was a living hell.

It had been a living hell for Timmy. Timmy was an eight year old physically and mentally impaired student in my school who lived in a wheel chair. Timmy had clear speech but a limited vocabulary that he used inappropriately. Of all the children in my school, I was strangely drawn to Timmy. He was a happy child with a sunny disposition. He crunched his eyes shut and rocked from side to side in his wheel chair, an absent-minded grin covering his face. He was always cooperative with his teachers. We all had a soft spot for him. One day, piqued by my fascination with Timmy, I pulled his file that dated all the way back to his birth. The medical reports confirmed that he had been born healthy. And the Child Protective Services reports confirmed that he had been battered during early infancy. Due to severe child abuse, Timmy sustained brain damage that rendered him deaf, blind and profoundly retarded.

I suddenly recalled another incident that occurred during my senior year in high school. When I was removed from my mother's custody I had only a few possessions. Among them, a handful of photographs, one when I was an infant and a few at age four or five, round-faced and always dressed in a plain-Jane dress. My mother parted my blonde hair down the middle, braided both sides, pulled the braids on top of my head and pinned them there. There were a few photos of her, the only visual memories that remained. I was taken away from her twelve years earlier at age six. If the rumors were true, I had surmised that her second child would now be around that same age.

One day I ran an errand to the post office. A cute little girl sat at the bottom of the steep steps that led up to the door. Something about her drew me closer. She had a round face and blue eyes. Then I noticed something very unusual, the girl's hair was braided and pinned to the top of her head. I halted for a moment. I had the eerie feeling that I was looking at myself as a six-year-old. We made small talk. The little girl was cradling a wounded butterfly in her hands, admiring the color in the butterfly's wings, "This butterfly is so pretty. I love butterflies and birds."

I asked, "What's your name?"

"Sally."

Lights flashed in my head. I knew that this was my half-sister. I recognized the hairdo. And she was wearing a dress, too, the same kind of plain dress, short sleeved, light blue, that buttoned down the back. The world began to spin. I registered, "This is my mother's other child. Oh, no! That means she has to be here someplace. I don't want her to see me. I don't want to see her. ..."

At that moment, Sally's mother came out of the post office. I nonchalantly stepped aside, pretending that I hadn't been talking to her child. I didn't want any part of making contact with her. But it was too late. I couldn't avoid being in her line of sight. She stopped alongside Sally, took her by the hand and said, "C'mon. Let's go!" She glanced at me offhandedly. I looked at her and froze, my eyes locked onto hers. I heard myself remark, "You have a beautiful daughter."

The woman said flatly, "Thank you very much." She didn't recognize me! Ironically, I was both incredibly thankful for and deeply saddened by it. Even though Sally looked like a happy, healthy child, I knew how awful her life had to be. But I pushed it to the back of my mind so that I could live with myself. That's where Sally stayed for the last dozen years, until now.

I received a phone call from a case worker who had been working with Sally for the last five years, "I was told by Sally's school that she had a half sister. Are you her half-sister?"

I took a deep breath. "Yes."

"I need to talk to you about Sally's situation. Her file

is six inches thick. Even so, we've never been able to prove child abuse. Now we have some evidence, human bites. A hearing's coming up to remove Sally from her home. Would you be willing to go to court and testify against your mother to support Sally's case?"

Not waiting for my answer, the case worker went on, "Since Sally's almost eighteen and incapable of caring for herself, she'll require a guardian. You're related to her and a professional in the field. Would you consider being Sally's legal guardian? She wouldn't have to live with you because she'll move to a group home with several other retarded adults in a sheltered environment. Your only responsibility would be to see that she gets the kind of program she needs and that her home is appropriate. Since she's financially supported by the state, you're other obligation would be to give her an allowance and pay the group home each month."

I was dumbfounded. Words escaped me. I could barely catch my breath. Guilt welled up again. I saw Sally on the post office steps years ago and was unable to help her then. Here was another opportunity. Maybe my help would liberate Sally; maybe it wouldn't. In any case I was clear about what I could and couldn't do for her. I couldn't go through the anguish of dredging up childhood memories by testifying against my mother in court, but for Sally's sake, I could consent to be her guardian, knowing that having a guardian lined up might help her to get out of her present circumstances.

At the hearing it was established that Sally would be removed from her home and placed in a group home.

Sally no longer resembled the small child on the post office steps, except for her clear blue eyes. She had matured into an attractive young lady. Her unkempt hair turned light brown and contrasted with her thick, dark eyebrows. She had a well-proportioned athletic body even though she walked with a slight halting gait.

For the first three months, Sally was in and out of several group homes. Every time her mother visited on Sunday afternoons, Sally displayed problem behavior for the next full week. Even though her mother abused her, she was the only parent Sally ever knew. Not understanding her change of environment, Sally threw violent and explosive temper tantrums and even ran away many times.

I worked with Sally's care providers to develop a tightly-structured behavioral plan for her, accounting for every minute of the day, both at home and in school. The plan outlined expected behaviors and consequences for non-compliance, such as not being allowed to go outside after dinner or no TV for three nights. It was absolutely necessary to adhere to this plan consistently, it was the only way to help Sally understand that her behavior carried consequences. We petitioned the court to drop maternal visitations for three months so that Sally could adjust to her new surroundings.

I liked Sally. I enjoyed as close a relationship with her as her capability would allow. I also understood her limitations. She didn't understand the concept of "sister," let alone "half-sister." To her, "guardian" meant that I was another person in charge, like a therapist or a teacher. Every few weeks I came to visit bringing her small gifts, a colorful pair of socks, or a new record, or her favorite butterscotch candies that she shared with the other residents of the group home. I brought her new barrettes because she enjoyed my brushing and styling her hair. Afterward, she preened in the mirror and showed off to the house mother. We went for walks outside and talked about boys and school.

As Sally settled into a routine at the group home, her behavior smoothed out. Violent outbursts dramatically reduced and periodic temper tantrums were dealt with consistently, evenly and predictably. Sally's positive behavior was acknowledged and lavishly praised. For instance, if she had no aggressive outbursts for a week, she was rewarded on the weekend with a special trip to the record store. She liked the other residents and her house mother, hugging them and freely engaging in household chores and activities. Eventually, she was able to work in a sheltered workshop where she fit drill bits, in ascending order of size, into their molded plastic boxes. She thrived in this environment. The work was highly-structured and repetitive. She was proud of her work, and especially proud of her paycheck. She spent it on records, perfume and teen magazines. Over time the visitations with her mother were slowly re-introduced.

Yet in all the years I would spend as Sally's legal guardian, I never once encountered, or even corresponded with, her mother. Ironically, she never attempted to contact me, until five years ago. In a letter she sent to me via my father she explained that she had breast cancer, "I don't expect to live much longer. I just want you to remember that I was your mother. Love, Mommy."

I had no reason to believe it because Mommy taught me how to lie as a toddler, to Dad and to the policemen. I asked my father to corroborate the story. "Do you think it's true?"

"No. Your mother lied about everything. Didn't you know she was crazy? She invented the world and made it the way she wanted it to be. She came from a poor, backward, uneducated family and had no idea how to be a wife or a mother. I even had to teach her how to change your diapers and how to hold you. She never believed that she was doing anything wrong to you."

I was struck by the pure coincidence of the whole thing. I was the principal of a school for trainable mentally impaired children. I had a half-sister in a school exactly like mine. My job was to develop specialized programs for people like her. What were the odds that Sally's only relative would be a professional in the field? It was so uncanny. No one would believe this story. Truth was really stranger than fiction.

9

Donovan
At The Door

With Darren long out of my life, I dated occasionally and admitted to myself that if the right man came along I'd be willing to meet him more than halfway. I wasn't dying for male companionship because my housemate Peter filled that role. Peter was the consistent male influence in Christian's life — not as a father, more like an older brother, a pal. He willingly assumed the day-to-day activities that living a life together entails. We went to the swimming hole, horseback riding, even took weekend trips together, as friends. Peter did chores around the farm, as a partner would. He helped select and plant trees on the property, painted and wallpapered, bathed Christian and put her to bed on the nights I had school meetings. We treasured a heartfelt friendship and a deep respect for one other.

The next Thanksgiving holiday we celebrated the farm's official "housewarming," even though we had lived there for three years. Peter and I planned four days of feasts and festivities for friends living all around the country. We arranged magnificent meals, brunches in the morning and theme feasts in the evening, an Oriental banquet, a seafood spread, and a traditional Thanksgiving supper. At any given time there were twenty people at the farmhouse. Some played cards, went horseback riding or hiked in the woods.

Peter often made references to his good friend, Donovan, whom I had met briefly in Colorado. Now that he lived north of Chicago, four hours away, we expected him to arrive any minute. I was sitting in the living room when Donovan arrived. Peter brought him around to meet everyone in the house. He was tall and lean with longish blond hair and a rugged yet sophisticated handsomeness. He wore blue jeans, a jean shirt and work boots. He walked in with an affable smile that never left his face the whole weekend. I noticed that he carried himself with a regal air of self-assuredness, without the usual attendant arrogance. He brought with him the latest portable radio tuned into the best local FM station.

I was instantly taken with him. He was interesting, neither shy nor reserved. He easily inserted himself in our home making himself and the other guests feel welcome. He roamed from one huddle of conversation to another, filling everyone's glasses. I followed him around as surreptitiously as possible, catching snippets of his descriptions of Egypt and the mysteries of the ancient pyramids. At the end of the evening, Christian went to bed and the party began to thin out. Donovan and I found each other alone in the sunroom. We talked about reincarnation, sports, out of body experiences, raising a child, psychic abilities, and professional achievements. Then Donovan asked the big question, "Do you like to travel?"

He lit my fuse: "I love to travel! But I've never had anyone to travel with. Where have you gone?" He sat at one end of the couch. I sat at the other, spellbound as he recounted his adventures all over the world. "How do you manage to travel like this?" I asked, "What do you do for a living?"

"I find a job that I like. Usually it has something to do with driving. Driving a truck, delivery van, courier, you name it. I stay with the job and save my money until I get the urge to travel again. Because my bosses usually won't give me the time off, I end up having to quit. Right now, I work in construction part time and live with my parents. My father is dying of colon cancer."

Something clicked between us, I could feel it. We talked until dawn. Reluctantly, I showed him to Christian's empty room. She slept in my room that night so that Donovan could have a guest room to himself. Quietly, I crawled into bed beside Christian and tried to sleep. But my head was swimming. I was wading into uncharted territory, captivated by an adventurer I hardly knew. The morning sky gleamed violet.

Later that morning, as we finished brunch dishes, Donovan received a phone call from his sister. His father's condition turned critical and he was admitted to the hospital. Donovan needed to go home. We caught each other's eye. It was obvious that he was enjoying himself and that leaving had not been part of his plans. I walked him to his car, carrying his portable radio, and offered, "Be sure to call us when you get home so we know you've made it all right. It's early in the weekend. If your father's situation stabilizes, we'd love to have you come back."

Early that afternoon, Donovan called to tell us that his father's condition had improved dramatically. "My dad asked, 'What are you doing here? I'm fine. Go back to your party in Michigan.' So put on a pot of coffee, I'll be there in four hours!"

I couldn't wait until he returned. I moved Christian back to her own room that night, just in case. For the next few days, we explored what was important to us. There were common threads that wove our lives together. It was clear that he was as attracted to me as I was to him. We both loved to travel, to experience the newness of being somewhere we'd never been before and to test ourselves in relationship to it. We were both attracted to the mystical aspects of the universe. Strangely, I had not revealed that side of myself to many people. With Donovan it was second nature.

By late Sunday, it seemed unnatural for Donovan to leave. I had found the other half of my treasure map. Our pieces fit together perfectly. We knew on a subconscious level that we would be walking through life's adventures together. We didn't have any evidence. But somehow we didn't need any evidence. For an hour he tried to leave, taking two steps out the door and one step back in. When he left I felt like a part of me, embodied in him, was absent. I longed to be with him.

I was intrigued by Donovan's close relationship with this family: his parents, his brother and sister, and his grandmother. Donovan's parents were his best friends. It seemed like a storybook tale to me, a total fantasy. When he talked about his father, I heard him swallow hard, "I took Dad for chemotherapy today. It makes me feel terrible to be so helpless. All I can do is drive as fast as I can so he can retch at home."

Donovan came from a family of doctors. His father was a cardiologist, his grandfather was a noted surgeon, and all of his uncles, on both sides of the family, were physicians as well. By contrast, Donovan didn't complete college. He was a free Spirit, and his family respected him and accepted him just the way he was, a trail blazer. I hadn't seen anything like it.

Over the next few months, Donovan came to visit on weekends as long as his father's health didn't require him at home. Since he hadn't been seriously involved with anyone for quite some time, his family was eager to meet me. I'd never met a family that wasn't dysfunctional, I was in the business of dysfunction. So meeting Donovan's family was like going to the zoo to see a rare species.

Donovan's mother, Marianne, was a slim woman of medium height. Her queenly presence belied her slight build. I liked her immediately. She was gregarious, easy to talk to and extremely direct. She needed to know every detail of my life. It was clear that I was being evaluated to determine if I were worthy of her son.

His father was lying in the back bedroom that had been converted into a hospital room. It smelled like a hospital, a musty heaviness laced with disinfectant. The image I had formed of him from Donovan's description was of a vital, rugged outdoorsman. I was unprepared for what I saw. I had seen disfigured and malformed people in my profession, but I'd never seen death. I had to collect myself.

Donovan's father looked skeletal, gray skin clung to his bones. I fought off queasiness and light-headedness and forced myself to smile, choking back tears. Although weak and feeble, his dark, sunken eyes penetrated into mine. He smiled at me. I knew how much he meant to Donovan and how much Donovan meant to him. Donovan introduced me, "Dad, this is Shari." I could tell that this was a familiar name to him. Even though he could barely speak, his long, trembling, bony fingers reached for my hand. To keep him from over-exerting, I moved my hands towards his and covered it with the warmth of my palms, "It's wonderful to finally meet you. I've heard so much about you."

In that instant I was overwhelmed by the "rightness" of this family. I held a boundless family unity in his failing grip. For the first time in my life, I recognized that families could be whole, even in the midst of profound grief. This family had chosen to keep their patriarch home, agreeing to do whatever it took to help him exit this life with grace and dignity.

Donovan loved Nana, his maternal grandmother. He spoke of her with tender respectfulness, "I picked up Nana from the beauty shop. We watched Jeopardy together. She's as smart as a whip for 85. I don't know how she stays in that big house all by herself." I was eager to meet her.

Nana lived only a few blocks away from Donovan's family. She came from a wealthy, aristocratic family. Her father was a famous Chicago politician in the 1930s. As we drove through an imposing gate and down a shaded drive, I could see her white, sprawling home that stood on the corner of her family's estate next to the lake. Donovan took me inside through the back door. The kitchen seemed plain and utilitarian, but the double doors pushed out into vast dining and living rooms. At one time, the house hosted lavish social gatherings that transformed the rooms into one giant ballroom. From my Amish perspective, it was a majestic museum. My eyes jumped from one precious specimen to another: pedestalled marble statues, a commanding oil painting of Nana's father, intricate hand-woven tapestries from Czechoslovakia, massive European antique furniture, thick Persian rugs and chandeliers.

I was breathless. Donovan, inured by the familiarity of it all, seemed impatient with my big-eyed wonder. He pulled me along excitedly, "C'mon, Nana's over there." Amidst all of this grandeur sat a diminutive woman, dwarfed by the scale of opulence and hunched a little at the shoulders. She wore a tasteful lavender dress, nylon stockings, and tiny pink slippers. Her short, dyed-dark hair was neatly styled. Everything about her exuded elegance. She held court.

Donovan kissed his grandmother on her cheek and chortled proudly, "This is Shari." He offered me a jade green overstuffed chair opposite Nana, while he scooted back to her side on the sofa. She smiled sweetly at me, obviously well aware of who I was. "Pleased to meet you," she said.

I replied, "The pleasure is all mine." I studied her closely. Nana was a proper woman, controlled in speech and movement. Both feet were placed on the floor and her hands rested on her lap, one perched on top of the other. Over the years an enormous diamond ring had carved a groove into her tiny finger.

Since her physician husband's death three decades earlier, Nana had lived alone. She was a wonderful woman, wise, non-judgmental, warm and loving, yet down-to-Earth. I was intrigued by the rich history of her life. Since Donovan had no interest in such things, she eagerly recounted details of helping her father entertain the literati of the day. She flipped through scrapbooks bulging with brittle, faded pictures and news clippings. I asked Nana if she'd like me to dust her curio cabinet stuffed with treasures from international excursions. She was impressed and flattered that I would volunteer to clean her precious possessions. But to me they were triggers to her stories. I held up an ornate bracelet with inlaid gemstone scarabs, "Nana, what's this? Where did you get it?"

"In 1924, my husband and I took a ship to Egypt. I picked it up from an open-air market in Cairo. Aren't the colors pretty?"

Nana lived a life on the opposite end of the social and economic spectrum from my own, yet she was a practical, unaffected, ordinary person. Her feelings about her life were the same as mine about my life. I learned that we all respond in similar ways to our circumstances, regardless of how meager or how privileged they are. I also realized that I didn't have to be circumscribed by the conditions of my early life. I could choose to be happy. I didn't need permission. I understood why Donovan loved Nana so much, the splendor that surrounded her was dwarfed by her personal magnificence.

Three weeks after our visit to Nana, Donovan's father died. After the funeral, Donovan came to visit for the weekend. He was grief-stricken and physically and emotionally exhausted. For the past year and a half he had worked only part time so that he could be available for his father's care. He had focused his whole life on his father. Now what?

Donovan told me about a tiny, quaint island off the coast of the Yucatan Peninsula, called "Isla Mujeres," offering crystal clear turquoise water and tropical sunshine, the perfect antidote for his grief. To travel now would jump-start his life of adventure again. We began making plans to take Christian with us and spend two months during the summer backpacking and visiting the Mayan ruins. It was my first trip out of the country.

I noticed something foreboding when we said "goodbye" to Marianne and Nana. Donovan, as usual, kissed Nana on the cheek. She smiled up at him and said, "Have a wonderful trip, Dear. Don't forget to send me a postcard." Then he kissed his mother, scooped her up and held her tightly. They broke into tears and stood, clinging to each other for several minutes. So many minutes, in fact, that I felt the need to give them a private moment to express their grief. Christian and I waited for him in the car.

A month into our trip, I was lying on the beach soaking up a rich, full-body, golden tan. Suddenly, I felt a strong impulse, "Donovan, I need to call home."

He laughed, and shrugged his shoulders, "Good luck. There's only one phone on the island and you usually have to wait a couple of hours to use it. So we better choose a time and go get in line ... Are you sure? Peter's taking care of everything."

After standing in line for two hours, I made a collect call to Peter from a tiny phone booth. Through the bad connection, he accepted the charges and yelled, "I'm so glad you called. I've been trying to figure out how in the world to get a hold of you!"

The line crackled in my ear. I shouted, "Why? What's wrong?"

Peter paused a moment, "Donovan's mother has died."

"No! You mean his grandmother," I shouted.

"No, his mother has died, M-O-T-H-E-R! Donovan's uncle called here trying to locate you." I turned around to look at Donovan who heard me shouting into the phone. His face was white.

Peter continued, "Have Donovan call Nana right away!"

I hung up the phone. There was no way to soften this, "Donovan, your mother has died. Please call Nana immediately."

Donovan reacted calmly. With a clear head, and on automatic pilot, he placed a call to his grandmother's house. His Uncle Paul, and anesthesiologist, answered the phone and accepted the charges. "You mother has expired."

"How?"

"Cardiac arrest. Because we were unable to reach you, we went ahead with funeral arrangements. It's scheduled for the day after tomorrow."

There was no time to waste. We spent the evening packing and the next day flew back to Chicago.

Uncle Paul picked us up at the airport and took us straight to the funeral home, "What's going to happen with the house?" he asked. "Who's going to sell the Winnebago? Who'll handle the legal affairs? What about your brother and sister?" The answer to all of the questions, of course, was Donovan.

Logistics were the farthest thing from his mind at this moment. Not in a million years did he ever anticipate receiving news like this. His uncle took Donovan aside and explained to him what had really happened, "Nana found her. Your mother took an overdose of sleeping pills. She was desperate. She didn't want to go on living without your dad. It looked like her children were taken care of. Your brother's married. Your sister's in college and you're happy in your new relationship. Why should she stay?"

At the funeral home, Donovan bent over the open casket and peered at his mother lying in state. She was as beautiful in death as she was in life. Each child put something special into her casket. Donovan pinned her favorite broach to the lapel of her suit. It was the lapis and silver pin that he had designed for her with a stone he bought in Egypt. Donovan's best friend, his mother, was gone.

His life collapsed. He had lost his father and his mother within a few months of one another. Shock and trauma overwhelmed him. He was distracted. He lost weight. I came to visit him on weekends to help him sort through the vestiges of his life. "Does this go to your brother? Does this go to your sister? Does this go to you?" He couldn't make a decision.

Although he remained loving and attentive to me, I realized that some part of the man that I fell in love with was gone, buried with his parents. I tried to convince myself that it wasn't really gone, just numbed, because every now and then I caught glimpses of his former playfulness.

For the next six months Donovan sorted through the maze of confusing details. What would he do next? Where would he live? How would he pick up the pieces? I was frightened that I was going to lose him. Would he want to live with a woman who had a child? I hoped so, but I didn't know for sure. Since he couldn't even sort through a pile of papers, how could he make a decision like that?

Somehow, through the fog of agonizing pain, Donovan found his way back to the farm.

10

The Spiritual Journey

The passing of Donovan's parents was the emotional dead of winter for him. Peter, Christian and I let him be. We knew that he would have to find his own way out of his grief. For our sakes he tried to muster an occasional smile and to resume some normal activity. To pass the time he worked around the farm mending fences, chopping wood, caring for the horses and building them an exercise arena. He got Christian ready for school in the morning and had dinner prepared when I came home from work in the evening.

Within a few months, Donovan ventured out by working part time for the farmer next door. Although he felt the need to make a financial contribution to the household, he didn't take the job solely for the money. He wanted to learn how to drive the tractor. It was another vehicle to master. It wasn't unusual for him to push the limits of his mind and body. Before we met, he had taken courses in mind expansion, astral projection, and psychic development. He explored consciousness as avidly as he explored the globe. He actually visited sites in Nazca and Macchu Picchu, Peru mentioned in Erich Von Daniken's book, *In Search of Ancient Gods.* Before he went to Egypt, Donovan read everything written on the mysteries of the ancient pyramids, including the writings of Edgar Cayce.

I also had developed an interest in Cayce's work so we planned a trip to Virginia Beach to the Association for Research and Enlightenment libraries, where original volumes of Cayce's actual psychic readings are on file. For four days over spring break we buried ourselves in research, looking up specific topics; headaches, ulcers, meditation, past lives and reincarnation. There, in the Cayce readings, was a statement that one of his patients would not be reincarnating back to this planet. If he weren't, then clearly I didn't have to either. Throughout my life I had a knowing, not confirmed by any conscious corroboration, that I would not come back to Earth after this life experience.

Edgar Cayce treated as natural that which I had always intuited. I'd never taken a metaphysical course yet I felt connected with the world as I perceived it through him. Out-of-body experiences seemed odd to most people, but Cayce treated them as commonplace, as he did the ability to perceive auras. His patients not only shared similar experiences which I thought were ordinary and natural, but there were books on the subject, libraries of them!

The Cayce research validated what my Grandma told me was real: There had to be more than this physical world. More than ever before my life was imbued with a sense of the mystical. The doors to my spiritual exploration were blown off their hinges.

Perhaps as a result of my heightened mysticism, I had an experience that opened wider my appreciation for the relatedness of all living things. It was asparagus picking time in early spring. Every year I looked forward to picking the first tender shoots of wild asparagus that popped up alongside the fence line in front of the farm. After school late one afternoon, I walked down the road with a gathering basket and sharp knife noticing golden sunlight dappling through the budding trees. The air smelled crisp and fresh as redwing blackbirds darted back and forth from the pond.

I spotted the telltale dried brown stalks from the year before. They pointed down to show where they had sprinkled their seeds. Even though the new grass was high along the fence, every serious asparagus hunter is willing to search on all fours. I spread the tall grass apart to spot four or five solid green spears protruding from the soft ground. I admired their perfection, leggy shoots of new spears next to their ancestors of dead stocks, a startling juxtaposition of life and death. I pondered how asparagus was created, how it grew, and how it regenerated itself. It seemed such a small thing among millions of things in creation, yet it had its own part, an invaluable part in the entire earthly construct. So did I. Weren't we magnificent, asparagus and I?

At that moment, I felt an energy zip through my body. Zing! I was inside the asparagus spear experiencing suspended animation. Then I heard a message, a deep powerful transmission decoded in every cell of my body, "We are all one, you know." Like Alice through the looking glass, I stayed tiny and green for what seemed like several seconds. Just as suddenly I snapped back to human form. But I could still feel the voice reverberating throughout my body, "We are all one, you know.... We are all one, you know."

Something awesome and mysterious had just happened. I could feel the transmission echoing inside my body for hours. I was so filled by the Spirit of the universe that I felt like Moses coming down from the mountain. When I walked back to the farmhouse, Donovan greeted me at the door, "You're positively glowing. And your basket's empty. What happened?"

"Something ... but I'm not exactly sure what. And it's still going through me. As soon as I can describe it I'll tell you about it."

I didn't understand what was meant by "We are all one, you know." There was no place in my studies about psychic phenomena or in my life's experience to insert this information. I began to read about practical spirituality, mysticism and the lives of the saints. I learned that we are spiritual beings having an earthly experience that includes past lives, coincidence, and the importance of the mundane, like picking asparagus. I shifted from focusing on what had been wrong with my life's experiences to what was right and useful about them.

For example, one warm summer Saturday, Dad and Beverly came to the farm to help us split fire wood for the winter. Dad enjoyed helping us with this all-day chore. Every year he hauled his hydraulic log-splitter to my farm to split a huge pile of hardwood logs that Donovan piled by the barn. Beverly stayed in the house with Christian, while Peter, Donovan and I formed an assembly line. We couldn't talk over the splitter's diesel engine, so I used this time to think about my father, as he positioned each log precisely on the splitter and pulled the handle to split it.

"How kind you can be. I've seen you be generous to other people. You are so knowledgeable about hunting and fishing and building and cutting wood. People always ask your advice. You loan the neighbors your tools. If you think they can't handle the job, you even do it for them. You're always available to help someone. That's why you're well liked. But why didn't you jump in? Why didn't you protect me? Your drinking destroyed whatever family we could have had. I can forgive you and forgive you and forgive you. But I can't get over being mad at you."

A couple of hours passed. Sweat soaked through our shirts. It was time for a beer. I carried a tray full of cold beers from the refrigerator, grumbling under my breath about giving alcohol to an addict, and about how obnoxious my father would get. Every time I saw him drinking it reminded me all over again how mad I was at him. Just then, in mid-step, with a powerful head of angry steam built up against him, a veil lifted. At that moment, I could sense his entire life. He was only capable of giving to me what had been given to him. He could only offer to me what was there to offer. Not my fantasy, not my hope, not my wish about what he should have been, good, right, loving, respectful, but what he actually was. It was time to stop blaming him for not being someone that he was not equipped to be. I was making myself miserable by wanting him to be different. And I was kidding myself by thinking that I could change him in any way.

Dad had the right to his own belief systems, his own problems, his own view of the world. He, like the rest of us, could only see through those filters. They were his unique perspective on the world. It wasn't mine. And it wasn't my preference. But there was nothing I could do about it. In that instant, not only did I forgive him, but I forgave myself for being angry with him. I realized that I was looking at him through the only filters available to me up to this point. There were no more expectations, no more overlays. It was a realization that went beyond forgiveness. Why did I have to forgive behavior that was already his highest possibility?

When I finally recognized my father as a fallible human being rather than an imperfect father, my relationship with him was transformed. Not because he did anything different, but because I was able to perceive him differently. He still frustrated me and I still chose not to be with him when he drank, but the resentment dissipated. This new perception would serve me in other areas of my life. All the poison that I swallowed about people and situations could be instantly neutralized.

To augment my academic as well as my spiritual growth, I continued taking professional enrichment courses at Michigan State University. In one class on releasing pain in the physical body, the professor applied new body work principles, cranial-sacral therapy, to the mentally impaired. From a traditional therapeutic perspective, we learned to scan the body with our hands to sense blocked energy, read it and re-direct that energy. Whatever we called it, it looked like laying on of hands, working with the healing forces of the universe. Are some people just natural-born healers or does everyone have the capability? Healing power seemed to be accessible to anyone who was open to receivership and open to being the instrument. But I didn't have any proof of it. The best way to find the answer was to be involved in it myself.

I kept going to class to open my healing channel even more and to receive a certificate of credibility, mostly to convince myself that I indeed possessed healing power. I had read stories of instantaneous healing so I knew that it was possible. I was eager to practice flowing energy, yet timid and shy about offering such strange-looking healing techniques in conservative, mainstream America.

Donovan, Christian and I went to visit Grandma and Grandpa one Sunday to pick strawberries. My father was there, complaining about bursitis in his hips and shoulders. He was clearly in a lot of pain. All of a sudden I felt my hands heat up as a powerful energy swept through me. Still, I was reluctant to tell my father that I could help him. What if he laughed at me? I didn't want to embarrass myself in front of my grandparents either. Meekly I offered, "I think I could help you with that. I'm taking a course at the University and I've learned some techniques that can ease pain."

He eagerly accepted, "I'll do anything to feel better."

By then my hands were burning. I laid them on his shoulder and, trying to deflect the attention somewhere else, said, "You don't have to do anything, just keep talking to Grandma and Grandpa. I'm just going to put my hands where it hurts."

My grandmother leaned over, and whispered very sweetly, as she always did, "Oh! Can you take pain away with your hands too?"

She saw the surprised look on my face and continued, "I could never explain how, but my hands got red and hot and I felt an urge to put them on someone who was ailing. I learned to do this at a very young age, but I never told anyone about it. I just figured that God wanted me to use my hands this way, so I did."

My mind raced backward. I wondered how many times over the last thirty years she had actually made me feel better when she touched me or hugged me. Especially coming from her, my first true spiritual mentor, her revelation validated the energy pulsing through my body and out my hands. I wasn't crazy. This was a very real and relevant form of healing. From then on, I freely worked with my hands, allowing myself to become an instrument for universal healing energy to flow through me.

I couldn't wait to share these techniques, in their traditional "medical" format, with the teachers and therapists at my school. I taught a workshop in which we demonstrated the techniques on one another. Usually there was immediate relief of any physical or emotional pain held in the body. The therapists wanted to incorporate this form of healing immediately in their sessions with our students.

I practiced on Gordon, an eight-year-old, severely multiply-impaired youngster. Even tempered and pleasant, he seldom cried or had emotional outbursts. I asked permission from his parents and from the superintendent even though I knew that this was a benign holistic treatment. Gordon's mother was very interested in our new therapy, especially because it seemed so simple.

I put Gordon on the therapy table and talked him through the procedure, even though it was clear that he could neither understand nor respond. After a few minutes of laying my hands on his chest, back and head, Gordon began to scream, shrieking at the top of his lungs, absolute bloody murder. I stopped working on him immediately. No one had ever heard him scream before. He cried and screamed inconsolably. Even though I held him and talked softly to him he carried on for three hours.

I tried to understand what happened. Somehow through the shrieks, I found myself communicating with him telepathically. His Spirit spoke to me, "Though you have unleashed all this emotion, I really didn't ask for it. You can't heal me, because I haven't requested it. I choose not to be changed in the way you think I should." He was right. There was only one person I forgot to ask, and that was Gordon. Because he looked like he couldn't even give permission, it never even occurred to me to ask for it. And I held an attachment to how he "should" be healed, never considering what might be perfect for his soul's development, regardless of his outward physical condition.

I was stupefied that I could have violated his sovereignty so blatantly. Gordon taught me an important lesson: unless there is a genuine invitation, *nothing* we offer to someone else is received or appropriate, even if we are convinced it's in their best interest. In our eagerness to share what has assisted us, we unconsciously impose ourselves on others by assuming that everyone would surely want the same thing, and that it would have the same positive effect in their lives. This subtle truth applies to giving advice, raising children, counseling, and even offering opinions. Even if someone consciously and verbally asks for help, their subconscious belief system may not allow them to receive it, or to receive it only to a limited degree. It's neither useful nor possible to cross another's "no trespassing" sign.

Every summer Donovan, Christian and I planned a two-month trip to an exotic place to experience adventures in contrast to our day-to-day lives. Always, a few weeks before it was time to come home, I felt resentful because it meant returning to "reality." I asked myself, "Why should I be tied to this schedule, nine-to-five, five days a week? I don't want to be married to my job. I want to enjoy the freedom of my time long before I retire." I mentally set a goal and added it to my dream list, "Take two years off." I didn't know how long it would take to achieve or when it would happen, but clearly the first step was to begin setting money aside.

We spent part of the next summer in the Ecuadorian Andes, amid the splendor of the mountains. We caught a rickety city bus that had been converted with train wheels to a makeshift railway car that edged its way up the mountain.

It pulled away from the station at 5:30 a.m. that freezing morning.

Excursions like these also helped me overcome my fear of heights. Our seven hour trip wound up and over the highest peaks in the Andes. As the "bus-train" chugged its way above the clouds, we could barely spy the city 9,000 feet below us. The more the train jostled and lurched its way along, the more nauseous I felt. At the mid-point of the journey, our young driver screeched to a stop on a steep incline. Built into the side of the mountain was a remote shrine to the Blessed Mother. He rolled down his window, dropped a few coins into the prayer box, crossed himself reverently and bowed his head in silent prayer. I was terrified. I knew what he was praying for. Several carcasses of trains like ours rusted in the ravine below.

My hands gripped the armrests, my shoulders hitched up around my ears. Too afraid to look down, I locked my eyes on the windshield stains. I was out of control. I couldn't deal with the terror of having my life in someone else's hands, the hands of a driver too young to be experienced and too insecure not to stop for prayers. I squeezed myself into a tight ball of fear, every muscle vigilant for the impending disaster. Then I realized that the ride would only get steeper as we picked our way to the top of the mountain. I could either sit there, paralyzed, for three more hours, or I could find some way to surrender to it. I opted for the latter, and closed my eyes, "Dear God, I give my life over to you. Thy will be done." I breathed deeply and fully for several minutes and felt my body relax a bit. I loosened my grip on the seat, shook out my shoulders, opened my eyes and smiled to Christian sitting beside me, "Great view from here, huh?"

At the top of the world the sun came up cloaked in

a rosy hue against a looming mountain peak that seemed to rise up like a citadel among the clouds. I was moved by its silent perfection, reminded that all was really right with the world. Although I felt dwarfed by its dimension, I felt augmented by its majesty. Because "We are all one, you know," its strength reflected my own.

Inside the coach, our breath seemed to hang in mid-air. A tiny wizened old woman ambled up the narrow center aisle selling piping hot hearth-baked potatoes. The earthy aroma of fresh potatoes wrapped in newspaper filled the air. I bought a steaming-hot potato and enveloped its newspaper skin with my frigid hands, soaking up the moist heat. Comfort food this high! I took three bites of the potato, savoring each mouthful. Then I looked down to see a half dozen brown worms, some still wriggling slightly, some fully baked. "Oh my God! Worms!" No one else on the crowded train seemed to notice that their potatoes might be riddled with them so why should I? I took a deep breath and kept eating, careful to bite around them. It was a poignant lesson on giving up the way things ought to be to allow grace enough to appreciate the way things really are.

Traveling expanded us beyond our own small world and our own small stories. Up to now I needed to control my world. As long as it was predictable, I was assured of being loved and not hurt and getting what I wanted. Traveling in Third World countries, nothing was under my control. I soon learned to give up controlling the way our trips had to be and learned to be flexible. Traveling became my boot camp for handling change, unpredictability and acclimation.

Our philosophy was, "the more money we spend on a plane ticket, the longer we should stay." We stretched our budget, turning on a dime with nine cents change, by

sleeping in less expensive hotels. We could make a comfortable environment anywhere we went, despite lack of creature
comforts. We didn't follow a set itinerary with a tour group
but rather always charted our own course, following hunches
and intuitions about what was in front of us every day.

We decided to stop off in Costa Rica for a month of
sunshine and sea on our way home. Costa Rica wasn't
called the "rich coast" for nothing. Days were typically
sunny and warm, an even 75° all year round. Deep lush
jungles met a crystal blue ocean along unspoiled beaches.
Toucans and scarlet macaws screeched from the dense
forests while troupes of monkeys swung from limb to limb.
It was a gardener's delight, hillsides blazed with orange-
flowered trees and delicate orchids hung high in the canopy.

The Costa Ricans were kind, friendly, helpful
people who loved to interact with Americans and deeply
appreciated our attempts to speak to them in their language.
They enjoyed a peaceful, democratic government that had
never gone to war. They had no army and their policemen
didn't even carry weapons. Costa Rica was an oasis of peace
amid a hotbed of political upheaval in Central America.

It was August. By now we had been there for two
weeks. We went for a walk on the beach with Julio, a young
Costa Rican man we had met two days before. When we
told him how much we loved Cost Rica he asked, "Why
don't you move here?"

As so often happened in my life, my mouth flew
open and I heard myself say, "We *are* going to move here."

Donovan and Christian both looked at me incredu-
lously and said in unison, "What?"

Disregarding their confusion Julio asked, "When?"

Again my mouth opened to answer, "January."

This time Donovan's mouth fell open, "We are?"

11

Costa Rica

We spent the next six months preparing ourselves. We sold the farm, the horses, the cars and almost all of the furniture. We kept a few favorite things and put them in storage at Dad and Beverly's house: family antiques, photographs, and Grandma's quilts. The timing was perfect for Peter who had fallen in love over the summer and wanted to move in with his girlfriend.

Leaving the States was bittersweet. I had spent only ten years in my profession. The principal of my own school, I thrived on the responsibility, interacting with the professional staff of teachers and therapists, the support we received from our administration, the satisfaction of providing the most innovative teaching techniques and watching our special students reach their highest potential.

Christian was 13, a gifted and popular child in an accelerated eighth grade class, who was busy with social activities. It was a difficult age to pull her out of school, out of her home, out of a secure life and plunge her into an unknown place, a place where they didn't even speak English. She wasn't thrilled with the idea.

Donovan, on the other hand, was thrilled with the idea, all aspects of it. Although he traveled extensively, he had never actually lived in another country, and Costa Rica was a beautiful choice. Everything about it aligned with his design — the weather, the natural beauty and the fact that it was still developing. Even the simplest things would be an adventure, like changing a light bulb. Where would we buy light bulbs? Are there hardware stores? What's the word for "light bulb?" What kinds of light bulbs do they use in Costa Rica?

During our preparations we frequently visited Nana on the weekends, spending as much time with her as we could before we left. One Saturday, I retired to my favorite bedroom to listen to music through the earphones of my cassette player. Suddenly, an intense brightness filled the room. I sensed a being at the source of the light that occupied the space from floor to ceiling. It was a fluid, gossamer, shimmery golden emanation. Out of the corner of my eye I saw three or four other radiant beings, identical to the central figure yet one-third its size. As the wispy golden being approached me where I sat on a bed, its smaller companions floated in and out of visibility. They seemed to migrate toward me from a place much deeper and much vaster than the physical dimensions of the bedroom. They expanded into every inch of space so that even the sensation of being in the room vanished.

I felt I was in a sacred presence. I could feel the intensity of their vibrations. An electrical charge prickled through my body, an electrifying case of the chills, a nuclear reaction on a cellular level.

I remember the thought, "I'm afraid I'll explode."

Almost as if they controlled my personal rheostat, the beings instantly adjusted their vibrational level to be more compatible with my own. I felt suspended in warm salt water, bathed in the infinity of God. It flowed over me, through me and inside me. It became me. There was no separation.

My eyes perceived everything as if they were wide open and yet they were closed. Hyper-aware, I melted into the golden radiance of those holy beings. My sense of hearing intensified in this ocean of silence. I heard a vast voice as expansive as its emanation, "We are always with you." I floated in the resonance of these words.

The principal being conversed with me telepathically for what seemed like hours, but probably was more likely only minutes. We dialogued with one another like two team members discussing the next play, exchanging ideas about a joint project. At the time, the interaction made sense and came to a natural completion. I sensed a sign-off like, "That's it for now." The glowing radiance departed as gracefully as it had emerged. I remember that as it began to fade so did the specifics of our interaction from my consciousness. But I knew that the feeling of integration, the warming of light, like caring arms folded around me, was imprinted in my memory. I was profoundly altered, left with an overwhelming sense of fathomless love, well-being and oneness.

More than ever before I was convinced that I was moving toward a deeper awareness of the divine. But my finite mind was perplexed, trying to make analytical sense out of the visitation, insisting on a rational explanation, while my heart willingly accepted the generous Spirit who filled my soul with waves of love.

The impact of my experience lasted for weeks. I was

convinced beyond a shadow of a doubt that my inner direction was on course, even though it looked capricious to others. Somehow, it felt right for us to go to Costa Rica, even though I had no practical answers to the questions from our family and friends:

"Why would you leave such a good job, mid-year?"
"What are you going to do there?"
"How are you going to live?"
"When are you coming back?"
"Where's Christian going to school?"
"How will you ensure that she'll get an equivalent education?"
"Why are you selling everything?"
"Why are you burning all your bridges?"
"What if you don't like it after a month?"

We had no idea how long we would be gone. We had no idea what would happen during the adventure. What we did know was that we weren't afraid to jump into it. We would come to live our lives like this, acting on our inner knowing instead of our mental, logical information. We would become accustomed to dealing with change and the unknown, and to follow this inner directive, no matter how illogical it appeared to others, or even to ourselves. It wasn't logical to quit my job, especially mid-year, and take Christian out of school to move to Costa Rica. But on January 15th, we landed in San Jose, the capitol of Costa Rica, with five suitcases and our German shepherd, Jesse. We brought lightweight clothes, tape players and cassettes, batteries and a re-charger, camera equipment and film, a tent and camping gear, masks, fins and snorkels, a large jar of peanut butter and a number of my favorite metaphysical, inspirational, and spiritual books.

We felt an urgency to get settled because there was

no place to board Jesse except with a veterinarian who kept him in an open arena full of sick dogs. Within five days we rented a three-bedroom stucco house in a quiet neighborhood on the outskirts of San Jose with a postage-stamp grassy courtyard in the middle and direct bus access to the city. We had no furniture, dishes, eating utensils, appliances or vehicle. Preferring mobility to acquisitiveness, we outfitted our house with only the basics: four plates, glasses and place settings of silverware. We bought an old, used four-wheel drive Land Cruiser we named, "Rattle Trap." San Jose is inland from the coast, so every weekend we safaried to the beach or went camping in remote areas, packing our food and equipment with us.

A top priority was to enroll Christian in school, but first we had to find one. She entered a private Costa Rican school and glided easily into her new academic and social surroundings. Gifted linguistically, Christian picked up Spanish very quickly. She rode the buses to anywhere in the city to meet her friends. She never complained about the changes in her life, even though adolescent hormones magnified her sadness about leaving her friends in the States and her self-consciousness about having long gangly legs.

Because I enjoyed walking around San Jose, I often walked the four or five blocks into the city. One day I passed a rickety faded wooden house set back a bit from the street. A small white sign tacked above the door read, "Téosofia." It didn't look like a residence and there were never any people there. I had a feeling that Téosofia could only mean one thing, even though the word wasn't in my Spanish dictionary — "theosophy." The Theosophical Society was founded in England by Madame Blavatsky in 1875. Its philosophy was based on mystical insights into the divine nature of man and the universe. I had devoured Madame Blavatsky's books for years and couldn't imagine that there would be a whole house devoted to theosophy in Costa Rica. If so, meetings might be held there.

One day I noticed a man carrying books up the steps of the old house. I approached him, searching my brain for the Spanish words, "Is this an organization?" The man barely understood what I was asking, but motioned me to come inside. Chairs were set up in a semi-circle around a presenter's table. The faint smell of incense clung to the air. He showed me an adjoining room that housed a small lending library of about a thousand titles. I scanned the Spanish words on their spines for any that I could recognize, especially the name, "Blavatsky." My heart raced. There it was!

I had enough command of Spanish to ask, "When do you meet?"

"Tuesday at 7:00."

Theosophical works were erudite enough in English, let alone in a foreign language. But I took the bus into San Jose for the meeting the following Tuesday. Thirty Costa Ricans had assembled there for over twenty years. For the most part they were in their fifties and sixties, except for two people in their early thirties, a Costa Rican man, Hernán, and myself. It was inconceivable to them that a blonde, blue-eyed young American woman would be interested in esoteric philosophy. They asked, "Who are you?" "What are you doing here?" "How did you find us?" "How long have you been interested in theosophy?" Before long I was regularly attending meetings conducted entirely in Spanish.

Hernán was a San Jose attorney who spoke conversational English. Through him I answered all of their questions and they answered mine. I became their pet. With Hernán by my side, the group always made sure that I knew what was happening. Each month the meetings featured a special theme facilitated by a member of the group who was an expert on that particular area of interest. Hernán's special interest was devas, or nature spirits, and angels. Someone else discussed esoteric geometry, the symbolism of ancient yet common symbols found in everyday life such as the triangle and five- and six-pointed stars.

I could intellectually grasp only 25 percent of what was discussed, and deciphering exhausted me. Finally one evening I just gave up trying to understand Spanish and allowed myself simply to hear the words and intuit the meaning. After meetings, I read about what we covered in *Key to Theosophy,* Blavatsky's book which I brought with me to Costa Rica. It seemed unusual to study the philosophies proffered by Blavatsky about the spiritual origin of man and the universe, and about world-wide ascended masters in a devoutly monotheistic Catholic country. But many Costa Ricans were exploring spiritual subjects and living a spiritual life while they quietly went about their daily routines. I met a past president of Costa Rica who had meditated with a large group of people for 25 years for world peace. Life for me in Costa Rica was a veritable smorgasbord of esoteric appetizers. I got involved in meditation techniques, Krishnamurti study groups, and the mystical teachings of the Kabala and Free Masonry. Sometimes Donovan joined me in activities which were of interest to him such as volunteering to work on special events for the University for Peace.

We remained in San Jose for nine months, taking advantage of its cultural amenities and exploring its rural areas within an hour of the city. We loved the fresh air and open spaces of the country where there was room for Jesse to run and big flower gardens. In the foothills of the Colón mountains we came upon a rental house with an impressive circular driveway that wound alongside a cream-colored stucco house with a red Mediterranean tile roof. The house was quite plain on the inside except for a dazzling little open-air sunroom off the back, closed in only by an iron grating. Since the property was unoccupied, we were able to rent it from the wealthy couple who bought it as an investment, and moved into it within two weeks. Christian even caught a bus from the house that took her to school.

Two days after we moved in, tragedy struck. We let Jesse outside in the morning, just as we always did. In the tall grass of the back yard he came upon a large poisonous frog that shot a milky white fluid into his face. Soon Jesse began convulsing. Twelve hours later he died in our arms. We were devastated. Jesse's death dampened the excitement of our move to this beautiful place. He was more than a pet, he was a member of the family. Most of all, he was Donovan's buddy. Donovan became despondent and withdrawn. For the first few days, we considered giving up living in Costa Rica and moving back to the States.

After about a week, we collected ourselves and chose to stay where we were. In Jesse's honor, we decided to build a boarding kennel for other expatriates' dogs and cats. We wanted to build the kind of kennel that we always looked for when we boarded our animals. Our landlords liked the idea. If we were building a business it meant we would likely stay. They assisted us by making referrals to local builders since it was difficult to find quality workers who spoke enough English to understand "cyclone fence" and "cement." Donovan immersed himself in the project, redesigning a large storage shed attached to the house with ten kennels big enough for Great Danes that opened up onto the fenced exercise area. Donovan enjoyed being "Jefe," the boss, coordinating all aspects of the job down to the small kennel doors. We named it, "Pura Vida Kennels," taken from a Costa Rican greeting loosely translated as, "Life is good."

Donovan and I shared the responsibilities of working with the animals. We asked veterinarians what Costa Ricans fed their pets since prepared food wasn't available. We cooked up our own stew concoction made up of chicken and beef parts, rice, a few vegetables and potatoes. The local English newspaper came out to do a cover story on "Pura Vida Kennels" that attracted customers from all over the city.

I took the bus into San Jose almost daily to attend spiritual study groups as well as the Theosophical Society. I listened to Hernán, who by now had become a friend, speak for hours about metaphysical subjects from a theosophical point of view. I especially liked his stories about the ascended masters, like Saint Germain, because I didn't know much about them. One day Hernán pulled a musty-smelling leather-bound book from his extensive library, flipped to a picture of Saint Germain and handed the book to me. I gazed at the oil painting rendition of a stately man. The details of his appearance were not as important as the familiarity of his presence, as if I had known him for lifetimes. I was stunned by the power of my recognition. It was almost like a reunion with a beloved relation. I trembled. Tears streamed down my face. I couldn't stop staring at the image, nor could I put the book down. His deep dark eyes looked like portals to the cosmos.

I discovered that Saint Germain was often referred to as the "Master Alchemist," the spiritual sponsor of

Freemasonry. Like the Master Jesus, he walked the planet in human form. There is actual documentation about his life in Europe during the time of the French Revolution. He was supposed to have lived many embodiments on the Earth plane, almost always among heads of state and secret societies, positively influencing political and social circles. It was said that he could dematerialize and assume the same form in other locations. As a famous alchemist, he transformed base metals into gold as a physical demonstration of how denser vibrations of consciousness can be transmuted.

From the first moment I saw his picture, I felt the presence of Saint Germain's energy. I came to realize that he was a presence that had been with me my whole life. The picture of Saint Germain resonated with the exact frequency of the golden being who had appeared to me in Nana's bedroom. I felt as if I had been re-connected with my all-loving benefactor.

South of the equator, it's summer from December through February. During her school break, Christian went with her friend's family to the beach for several weeks. Without her, Donovan felt as though the house were empty. In the silence, he also felt the deep wound of Jesse's death which re-catalyzed his grief over his parents' deaths. It was the deepest, most gut-wrenching grief I had ever seen. It had been five years since Donovan's parents died. I remembered from a college course on death and dying that people sometimes don't emerge from their grief until long after their loss.

Donovan was literally immobilized. He couldn't eat. He lay in bed until late into the afternoon, apologizing for his helplessness. One day I heard the shower running and running. I went in to check on him and saw him standing under the torrents of water, crying, "It hurts so much."

I tried to help him, "Don't worry about anything. I can take care of everything. You just try to get through this." I stood by Donovan's side while he grieved from the depths of his soul. Feeling his despair I cried with him and ached for his pain. At least he was expressing it. Still, I felt helpless. His painful paralysis lasted for three weeks.

One night we lay on the bed side by side. I read a book on the wild West and Donovan listened to his favorite music through the headphones of his cassette player. All of a sudden he sat straight up, threw off the headphones and grabbed my arm. It startled me. In a loud voice he exclaimed, "I see the light! I see the light at the end of this tunnel I've been in for so long!" He was finally able to put into words how sad and angry he was that his best friends left him, his father, his mother and our dog, Jesse. By doing so, they denied him the opportunity of sharing the adventure of his life with them. Because he couldn't express his feelings, he pushed them deeper inside him into the blackness of the void.

For the first time in five years, Donovan's head rose above the fog of emotional numbness. It was as if he had just returned from a long trip. "Where have I been all this time? What have I been doing? What have I been like to be with?" he asked. He was concerned that he had been too grumpy, distant and difficult. I hadn't seen this Donovan in five years.

Soon afterward Donovan had another revelation, "We have to go home, go back to the States." For five years his life had been unraveling. He wanted to pick up the loose ends and wind them back into a tight ball, to reclaim the part of him that was buried with his parents.

I didn't respond at all. I just smiled and let him talk about the future. But his proclamation launched an internal struggle for me. I didn't want to leave Costa Rica and I didn't want to tell him so. No matter how much I wanted to stay, I would never cast a shadow on his emerging light of hope. I said nothing for several days. When Christian returned from the beach we presented the idea to her, careful not to impose yet another change on her life. She had her bags packed before we finished the sentence. It was clear that she had missed her life back home.

I loved my life in Costa Rica! I felt lucky to live in this beautiful country with friends, hibiscus bushes and the sea. I was involved in several projects that were in the middle of things. In three weeks we were bringing in the head of the Theosophical Society of India to make a presentation at the University for Peace, and I was next up to facilitate one of my meditation groups. Finally, I had to admit that I just wasn't ready to leave. I asked Christian and Donovan to give me a month to sort things out. "If I'm not ready to go back by the end of the month, you two can go back and I'll join you whenever I can." It wasn't easy. Nothing was more precious to me than the two of them. I knew that Christian and Donovan had a destiny to fulfill, but so did I. Hard as it was, I had to honor my own life. I said a little prayer, "Dearest beloved Spirit of God, help me to see what is mine to do here."

Naturally, within a month, all of my projects came to a close. Every one of them. I was complete. Once again we sold all of our belongings. We met some Swiss people who had just moved to Costa Rica and made an instant connection with them. When they found out that it was time for us to leave, they bought everything we had, from the Toyota Land Cruiser to the silverware — every single household item. The proceeds from the liquidation would help us to re-establish ourselves back in the States.

We made the rounds, saying "good-bye" to all of our friends. When they asked, "Why are you going back?" my mouth flew open and I heard myself say, "We're going home to build a new world."

I looked around wondering, "Who said that? What does it mean? Here we go again... Now I get to find out what 'a new world' is..."

12

Montana

By early spring we returned to Michigan with money still left in our bank account. We had saved every penny for several years before leaving for Costa Rica, and our living expenses there had been modest. With those savings, combined with the money from the liquidation of our household goods, we bought a used, white Nissan Sentra and camping gear in preparation for the next adventure.

Christian had already completed her freshman year of high school in Costa Rica, so we weren't too rushed to find a home. When I was her age, I made a trip out West with Dad and Beverly. I was especially impressed by Montana's pioneer Spirit and geographic beauty, dramatic mountains, natural streams and plentiful wildlife. Donovan, interested in settling in the wild West, began pouring over Montana maps. Although we didn't know exactly where we would end up in Montana, we were confident that we'd recognize it the minute we saw it. There were only two criteria: the place had to be beautiful and we had to be able to find work there.

We loaded the car with our clothes and camping gear and wheeled westward into the sunset, visiting Yellowstone National Park and friends along the way. We drove all over Montana, exploring the places we thought we might like, discounting one after the other. "Nope, this isn't it." "No, this isn't it either."

A month passed. We were disheartened, frustrated and tired of camping. A real vacation would help us clear our heads, so we headed for the canyon lands of Utah. We hiked in the canyons and relaxed in the hotel pools. After a week we decided to return to Montana, to the place we had liked the best so far, even though it wasn't exactly what we wanted. Donovan charted a new route through a stretch of Wyoming to what seemed to be the back door of Montana. We came over a hill, known as the East Bench, and there it was! The stunning vista compelled us to stop the car. There in the valley below was a jewel of a small town. We could see vestiges of homesteaders' log cabins. Green meadows escorted a crystal blue creek through town out to endless snow-capped mountain peaks.

We looked at one another and instantly knew! Eureka! We headed down the hill to town and drove slowly along the three-block main street, admiring original old-West facades. The Red Lodge Chamber of Commerce could tell us how much sunshine to expect. Old Man Winter had just dumped six feet of snow, common even for May. Despite the snowy winters at 5,500 feet, we were guaranteed 75 percent sunshine.

We stayed in a local guest house for two weeks while we looked for a home to rent and a four-wheel drive vehicle. We met Steven, a realtor, who had just moved to his new home in the country. We rented his recently-remodeled house in town. Christian enrolled in the local high school to begin classes in the fall. We took the summer to return to Michigan to retrieve our few belongings from Dad's house, sharing with him our adventures in Costa Rica and new ones to come in Montana. He was glad to have us back in the country. Nana was glad too. As charming as ever, she still lived in her big house among the precious memories of her life.

Donovan immediately got a job at the local ski area. I couldn't see myself going back into education, especially in a small town with few professional opportunities. So I gave myself time to discover my next career. In the meantime, I took a sales clerk job in the downtown ski shop.

Our beautiful little town only had 1,700 friendly denizens. When we walked down the street everyone said "Hello." Since locals always spoke first, we could tell who was an out-of-towner because they didn't initiate the greetings. I enjoyed the cross-section of people: native ranchers and cowboys along with imports from other areas of the country, all with varied interests. Montana offered big game hunting, skiing, kayaking, mountain climbing and golfing. I kept an eye out for spiritual pals, but didn't recognize any. Feeling isolated, I put an ad in the local paper inviting anyone interested to join me in a meditation group. The only response I got was a crank call from our friend Steven who disguised his voice as an East Indian Yogi.

Even so, I never regretted the move to Montana. In Costa Rica I engaged in a daily life of rich spiritual investigation. But life wasn't about investigation, it was about living. It was one thing to go to a meditation class and bathe in the expansive group energy, but the idea was to extrapolate that energy into my everyday life. Spiritual practice wasn't something I did with like-minded people at a scheduled time; it was a way of *being* no matter where or how I lived, or with whom.

It was off-season at the ski shop. One particularly quiet day, no one had been in for several hours. I had time to dust and stock the shelves, sweep the floor and clean the windows. Then I had time on my hands. It was late afternoon and the low-hung sun streamed brightly through the window and warmed the heavy, solid-oak counter. It was too inviting. Like a lazy cat I hopped up on the counter to soak up the rays, and slowly closed my eyes, dangling my feet over the edge.

Snap! Just like that I was transported into a different scene in the same shop. This time I stood behind the counter. Two older-looking men, dressed in white garments, appeared in front of the counter. One was slightly taller than the other. He had free-form, chin-length white hair and a beard. His erect posture and a noble bearing imbued him with a commanding presence. His warm yet penetrating eyes seemed to reflect the wisdom of the world.

The other man, slightly shorter, had bushy white eyebrows and wavy but thinning white hair that met the top of his ears. A blissful half-smile curved around his face. His tranquil presence seemed softer than his stern-looking companion.

Without their mouths moving they spoke the same words simultaneously and directly into my mind. I know we carried on an intelligent conversation, but all I could remember were the words, "We wish to welcome you."

In a blink of an eye they disappeared.

I opened my eyes. There I was, still sitting on the sunny counter, dangling my legs. I wanted to kid myself and say, "Oh, you just fell asleep for a minute." But the two figures were real; the words they spoke were a real, tangible message. Yet I had no proof, no physical evidence. And almost no conscious memory of what they said beyond their greeting.

I'd never seen these men before, but they seemed strangely familiar. It was as if they were a greeting party. But who were they? Why were they welcoming me to Montana? I comforted myself with the knowledge that whoever they were their purpose would be revealed to me when they wanted me to know. As I thought about their visit, I felt as if invisible strings were pulling me toward further spiritual discovery. It was both a sober and thrilling reflection.

While I was preoccupied more and more with the spiritual magnetism of the messengers who came to me, practical concerns occupied my days. During my year at the ski shop, I was introduced to the concept of sales representatives and wholesale selling. Donovan and I liked the idea because it was both lucrative and flexible enough to suit our lifestyle. We started our own sales rep business in wholesale floral supplies and gifts. We made an arrangement with a reputable floral supply company and helped local artisans to develop entire gift lines to sell to florists, gift shops and drug stores in every little burg in Montana. We loved this business and liked interacting with our customers. Though my purpose for being with them included selling products and making commissions, I spent most of my time making friends with people all over the state.

Each of us was gone one week and home the next. On our off-times we hiked, fished, skied and traveled. We also bought a spacious four-bedroom home with a daylight basement. Although it was on less than an acre and had no trees on the property, we knew it would be a solid investment. Large windows framed a view of Mt. Maurice, the local ski area and West Fork Canyon. The house was close enough to town so that Christian could drive back and forth to school activities, yet far enough in the country that deer, moose, bear and even a mountain lion visited us.

Soon Donovan and I met enough like-minded people to start a small weekly meditation group. Every now and then we taught workshops on meditation and metaphysical subjects. We came out of our spiritual closet in the midst of a very conservative social environment.

By now, Donovan and I had shared a life together for seven years. Like most partners who are tuned in to one another, we completed each other's sentences and often found ourselves thinking about the same things. One day I asked him, "Honey, I've been thinking about something. How do you feel about getting married?"

He replied, as if he had been mulling over the same question, "You know, I've been thinking about the same thing lately. I've even planned a little get-away for the wedding."

Up to now there hadn't seemed to be a point in getting married since we were doing fine just the way we were. Although we couldn't imagine that marriage would have a significant impact on our relationship, we felt the impulse that now was the time. It just seemed appropriate. We opted for a small intimate ceremony in the Black Hills of South Dakota. Donovan's sister and her husband joined us. She honored the traditions of the ceremony by giving me something old, a beautiful garnet necklace that had belonged to Nana, and something borrowed, her own wedding dress. One sunny Thursday afternoon in a picturesque canyon, Christian stood next to us while we repeated our vows in front of the Justice of the Peace.

It was a simple ceremony, reflecting the genuine

love and commitment we felt for each other. By the time we got back to Montana we realized that our relationship really did change as a result. It wasn't because of the vows or the ceremony, but rather the declaration to the world that we were present for one another forever. Our love was truly deepened and spiritualized. To this day, we celebrate our anniversary on the day we knew we would become life partners, the day we met at the farm, Thanksgiving.

That summer Donovan and I went on a small honeymoon, a private week away together while Christian stayed behind in Montana with a friend. We went to Donovan's family's summer cabin in northern Wisconsin. It sat between two lakes, half a mile into a deep woods. Donovan's father built it for the family years earlier. Although we called it a "cabin," it was more accurately described as a small home with all the modern conveniences.

One lazy August afternoon, a cacophony of chirps and ribbets emanating from the lakes drifted in the dense air through the house. Donovan snoozed lazily on the sun porch. I propped myself up on the sofa in the living room reading an engrossing book about Marco Polo. Enervated by the heat and humidity, I put the book down and closed my eyes, tracing in my head the colorful journey the explorer had undertaken. All at once a familiar tingling of prickly chills swept over me. I thought, "I know this feeling." My eyes remained closed, yet I was keenly aware of my surroundings. The radiant, gossamer, golden being who had visited me before appeared again, this time flanked by two slightly smaller but identical companions. They emerged from a deep plane, as if a portal opened up in some far dimension. I tingled as they approached me.

My rheostat automatically adjusted, synchronizing

with their brilliant light and the all-loving vibration that came from them. I was ecstatic to be reunited with them. They said quite simply, "Now is the time. We want to take you on a journey." Thrilled with anticipation, I found myself gently rising up out of my body while the two shimmery attendants stood abreast of me and the largest one held my elbows and braced me from behind. I sank into the oneness fully guided and supported. We floated slowly inside the house and out through the roof. I thought, "We really *are* going somewhere."

At warp speed we darted in and out of different dimensions of space and time. My escorts, veritable tour guides of the universe, pointed out highlights along the way. We passed through a pocket of space and paused amid an overwhelming tone that seemed to echo through the universe. It was a steady, magnificent cosmic hum, a vast all-encompassing reverberation. I could hear it. I could feel it. I could breathe it. Its vastness intimidated me. "I'm going to explode in this sound." I remember thinking, "Help me to surrender." Instantly, my request was granted. The intense cosmic hum transformed into a sweet river of sound. "What is this? What am I hearing?"

"You are hearing the sound of creation," came the answer. "The sound of ALL THAT IS. The sound of God. The sound of OM." Even though I didn't understand exactly what it meant, I melted into its sweetness, a tantalizing immersion into infinite oneness.

Then, in a flash, we swooped in and out of realities. My escorts continued to explain, "All of existence is energy, a fluid flow of energy. On planet Earth you work with it by holding in your consciousness a congealed form of it which is called 'third dimensional reality.'" Then they projected images in my brain like a motion picture screen. I understood that my own fluid energy formed my physical body as I knew it and that my consciousness continued to hold it in that form. Energy, I suddenly understood, can coalesce into any form that the mind can conceive.

I was offered an image of our planet, the blue planet Earth. As if I were equipped with a powerful telescope, I zoomed in on aspects of life here that are held in form exactly the same way: a rain forest, a school, a crowded city, a desert, daily life of hustle and bustle, even destruction and war. From this perspective, I could see that all of it was a fluid flow of energy. My escorts explained, "This energy is the essence of God. It's what you call 'light.'"

I caught glimpses of other planetary bodies, but didn't recognize them as the planets in our solar system. Telescoping in on them I could see that they were alive, pulsating with the same universal creative energy and unique life forms of their own. Then, my escorts interrupted my fascination. "It's time to return," they said.

Not ready to end the adventure I asked, "While we're out and about, could we just check on Christian?" Even though my escorts had no visible form, I could sense them smiling. Here they were showing me the cosmos and I wanted to see my child. How human of me.

They lovingly honored my request. "We want you to know how easily this is done." Instantly, through my cosmic X-ray eyes, I peered into the house in Montana where Christian was staying. She and her friend were sitting on their beds talking and giggling. She was fine.

I opened my eyes, recognizing the familiar cabin in Wisconsin. I hadn't moved a muscle. Donovan still dozed quietly on the sun porch. Thirty minutes must have elapsed. I was profoundly grateful to have glimpsed the universe and to have heard the river of pure positive energy that hums throughout the cosmos. Because I didn't fully understand all the aspects of the journey, I shared this story with no one, not even Donovan, for several years. Trying to reduce the experience to words somehow diminished its impact. I cherished it within my being, secure that I would continue to grow into its fullness.

I discovered on that remarkable journey that we are not human beings having a physical experience as much as we are spiritual beings having a human experience. I also discovered that my community included much more than my back yard, even my planet. I finally understood too, that in my own truth, God, ALL THAT IS, the Oneness, whatever we call it, is not outside of me. God consciousness is embodied in my very existence. A spark of divinity lives inside me. Not only in me, but in all things in the universe and in all other universes. From that moment on, my prayers changed. I referred to God, not as an entity outside myself, not as an external authority who could save me, or grant or refuse my wishes, but as an aspect of myself: "Spirit of God presence that I AM, help me to understand." My sense of separateness began to dissolve.

I knew deep in my heart that the marvelous journey I had taken was not the main event. It was more like a short orientation course, a familiarization flight into the grandness of the universe. It was as if somebody had whispered in my ear, "you cannot take in everything at once. The glory is far too expansive. We'll show you enough to open your eyes so that you may see beyond yourself."

Later that summer, filled with an intense desire to learn more about the unusual experiences I was having, I perused the titles in our personal library to find something on a spiritual topic that I hadn't yet read. The library included 50 years' worth of National Geographic magazines, and hundreds of titles: coffee table books on exotic places, books on flower gardens, alternative healing techniques, an assortment of metaphysical topics, books on the saints and ascended masters and travel books. Among the books that Donovan contributed to the collection was *Autobiography of a Yogi* by Paramahansa Yogananda. I pulled it from the shelf and brought it outside to read in the sun that cut through the deck railing, casting ribbons of shadows around my bare legs. Engrossed in the book, the hours passed quickly. I looked up and noticed that the shadow ribbons had fallen completely away.

Absently, I turned the page to see a picture of Yogananda's guru Sri Yukteswar. I couldn't believe my eyes! My heart leapt up to my throat! He was one of the figures who visited me that day in the ski shop! I read on, feverishly, well into the night. On page 375, I came upon a picture of Lahiri Mahasaya, Sri Yukteswar's guru. He was the other figure who visited me in the ski shop! Nearly six months had passed since then. I had had no idea who these men were. I simply thought that they were two messengers who had taken on the assignment to welcome me to Montana. I was thunderstruck to see their faces between the covers of this book.

Needless to say, I savored each morsel of information. I soaked it up. Donovan suggested that I contact Yogananda's organization, The Self-Realization Fellowship, to get copies of his complete teachings. I also ordered everything I could from Ananda, an intentional community located in Northern California established by one of his devotees. Donovan had spent a week at Ananda learning about Yogananda's practical teachings on how to live a spiritualized life. I immersed myself in Yogananda's teachings. Although I loved everything he wrote, the most precious time for me was spent in meditation, allowing myself to feel the presence of this line of masters.

Of course, it was inevitable, according to Donovan, who was never surprised by the direction my spiritual education was taking, that I should go to India with the Ananda group. It was an expensive month-long trip and we could use the $3,000 to pay for Christian's college expenses. I vacillated, continuing to mull it over during my next week-long business trip.

Donovan's logic was overwhelming: "You can't put a price on something like this. Don't worry about the money. It'll all work out."

I left for India two months later with 29 other pilgrims from all over the United States. We came from various backgrounds and professions — from bankers to tree toppers. We were black, white, old, young, male and female. Many lived in the Ananda community, and all had one thing in common, a love for Yogananda's pathway that explained the purpose of life as evolution of mortal consciousness into God consciousness.

For the first time in my life, I didn't have to think about day-to-day necessities, hotels, meals or transportation. We were shuttled from one site to another and stayed in comfortable accommodations throughout India. I was free to totally immerse myself in the spiritual pilgrimage. We visited holy cities and sacred temples where untold numbers of followers had made similar pilgrimages of pure devotion. We walked in the footsteps of the masters, visiting ashrams and temples associated with each one. We saw Yogananda's boyhood home where he spent hours upon hours chanting and meditating in the celebration of Spirit.

We also chanted and meditated in each holy location in order to absorb sacred vibrations, the divine frequencies imprinted by thousands of daily supplicants. We commingled our energies with theirs. We walked and prayed and meditated and chanted and laughed and explored for 30 days. I was filled with gratitude for the opportunity to bathe in the radiance of the masters.

A large percentage of our group experienced culture shock in India. Because I had traveled to Third World countries I had seen poverty before. I looked at it from two levels. Although the external pervasive impoverishment was real, somehow a sacred, holy devotion permeated it. Instead, I went through culture shock when I returned home. It was a difficult re-entry. I had changed in a profound way that even I couldn't understand. I struggled to share my experiences and my reactions to them with Donovan, Christian and close friends, but could never truly relate what exactly happened.

I sank into depression. I couldn't function well. I didn't know how to assimilate the experience and apply it to my daily life. I was homesick for India. Face to face with my loneliness, I withdrew into my meditation room for several weeks. I called a few of my traveling companions consoled by the fact that some of them were going through the same thing. Only they could really understand how I was feeling.

I picked up *Autobiography of a Yogi* once again, hoping that I could find comfort in its pages. I remembered that Lahiri Mahasaya and Sri Yukteswar said in the ski shop that day, "We wish to welcome you." *What* were they welcoming me to? I didn't want to embrace only one path. I wanted to be a spiritual seeker selecting pieces from various disciplines and distilling the essence that was true for me to create my own spiritual reality. I followed in the footsteps of the Masters because they cut the path of consciousness but I also wanted to walk beside them along my *own* path.

As I read about Lahiri's life, the dichotomy began to make sense. Lahiri was called a "householder," which meant that he wasn't alone in an ashram or a cave living the ascetic life. Rather, he had a family, and a job, as well as initiating many people into Kriya Yoga. After he made a spiritual pilgrimage to his master, Babaji, he overflowed with the ecstasy of God presence. Babaji told him that his mission was to return to the world and that many seekers would come to him because he could meet them at a place they understood, in their humanity. Lahiri explained, "Firmly anchored in the Spirit, again I assumed the manifold family and business obligations of a householder."

It dawned on me that being filled with Spirit represents heaven and our "household" life represents Earth. Inspired by Lahiri's understanding of his unique gift of God, I wrote a similar declaration and placed it on the altar in my meditation room, "Firmly anchored in Spirit, I now return to my day-to-day life." I finally understood that to be effective as a spiritual human was to apply a reflected goodness of God in daily life — as a householder. The two masters, Lahiri Mahasaya and Sri Yukteswar, were welcoming me to my divine purpose, a bridge between heaven and Earth.

While I was establishing the spiritual link to God, our wholesale business in Montana continued to expand. Donovan and I had built a solid reputation with our customers, who looked forward to our regular visits and counted on the new and different merchandise we carried. The business was running so well that it no longer required my full-time attention. As a matter of fact, it was becoming repetitive, offering no new challenges.

Using the additional energy and time available, we

developed and facilitated weekend workshops: *The Joy of Meditation, The Gift of Life, Living the Life that You Were Intended to Live,* and *Exploring Who You Are as a Universal Being.* We held spiritual counseling sessions for private clients, helping them to move through dysfunctional behavior patterns created by their closely-held belief systems, assisting them to bring into their lives more of that which they truly wanted, and guiding them to perceive new ways of living and new possibilities for their lives. This work was innately interesting to us because it was in perfect alignment with our spiritual values.

Living in Montana for six years, Donovan and I began to feel a stirring. All areas of our lives seemed complete. Christian was in her second year of college, two-and-a-half hours from home. Her life was stable and goal-oriented. The business was solid and thriving. I felt like it was time to move on to the next thing. But what?

As we pondered our future, some friends, Kathleen and Robert, invited us to visit them in Washington State. We had met them at a spiritual workshop in Arizona eight months earlier and instantly liked them. Kathleen was a tall, beautiful, fair, graceful woman who carried herself with a regal elegance, like an empress. We shared a deep, abiding love and appreciation for the mystical nature of life. Every moment her mind was filled with exploration, discovery and revelation. I loved that. I also loved her fascination with horses, training them and riding them English style. She was the minister of a new-thought church as well as a conscious channel, opening herself as an instrument and a mouthpiece for divine messages and inspiration.

Her husband, Robert, was an energetic, effervescent and dramatic man with a glint in his eye and a shiny bald head which he kept shaved cleanly. He had an entrepreneurial Spirit, always dabbling in some kind of business venture. A bon vivant, Robert talked about interesting things, mostly his next project, with marvelous story-telling abilities. We looked forward to our two-week vacation with them to explore the Pacific Northwest.

On the drive across Montana Donovan asked, "Would you ever consider living in Washington?"

"Absolutely not! That climate would never agree with me."

We ended up spending three weeks there. On a crisp October morning I brought a cup of tea out to Kathleen on the deck and sat on the railing breathing in the early-morning dewy smell. I looked out at her graceful horses grazing in the field. Majestic Mount Rainier loomed in the background. I began to recite to her all of the reasons why I shouldn't move to Washington, "I love Montana so much. I have a body and temperament that are nurtured by the sun. It doesn't look like there's as much sun here as I need. And Christian's in college back in Montana."

Kathleen said, "Why are you giving me a laundry list about why you shouldn't move to Washington? No one has told you that you *have* to."

I had no answer. I didn't know. It was as if I had to make a case against the inevitable. A few days later, driving through the lush green countryside, Donovan and I looked at one another and said almost simultaneously, "We're moving here, aren't we?"

We were totally drawn by our spirits to make this move. It was clearly the next thing to do. By now we were accustomed to making split-second, life-changing deci-sions. We thrilled at the thought of a brand new adventure, yet sighed at the sadness of leaving Montana.

13

The
Walk-Out

We arrived home on Thursday night and prepared to leave Montana immediately. On Friday, the realtor listed our house. Donovan mentioned our move to the lady in the bakery who came out to look at it that night. By Monday we had an acceptable offer. We couldn't help but notice the extraordinary circumstances that accelerated our moving plans. Spirit truly does work in strange ways. We had 60 days to close escrow, pack and move to Washington.

In the meantime, we were scheduled to go to Casper, Wyoming to visit friends and hold some spiritual counseling sessions at their home. Even though it was in the middle of our feverish rush to move, we wanted to honor the commitment we made to them. Sylvia and John were our summertime neighbors. They owned vacation property on the river near our home where they had put up a Mongolian yurt. It was a magnificent, nature-filled retreat. Pots of flowers dotted the wooden wrap-around deck and handsome handmade bird houses peeked through the trees. Neat paths wound their way through the woods to the sparkling creek. The yurt had an out-in-the-wilderness feeling, yet it generously offered all of the comforts of home. We visited Sylvia and John frequently during their vacations from teaching school. We shared interests in living a mobile, almost nomadic life and pursuing spiritual growth.

John came from a Wyoming ranching heritage. He was strong and masculine, yet tender and soft at the same time. I tried to imagine him as a typical rancher. Although he was outdoorsy, he was also interested in speaking thoughtfully about metaphysics. He was a kind and warm man, an avid information seeker on just about everything. For example, he investigated all the companies that produced yurts to find the best value at the best buy. At one time I mentioned to him that I might be interested in starting a guest ranch. He already had files of information on how to do that. He engaged us for hours talking about his varied interests.

Sylvia, a nurturing, loving woman was the total embodiment of feminine attributes. She was both an elementary school teacher and an accomplished hands-on energy healer. Every moment of her life was infused with a sense of the sacred. She made sense of her life's events by filtering them through her keen spiritual understanding. She studied the subtle dynamics of interactions between people and the impact of belief systems on human behavior, relating it all to the divine perfection of the universe. Sylvia always seemed to know what worked and didn't work for her, and what was true and not true for her. She also allowed others to live their own truth.

John and Sylvia owned a sprawling winter home in Casper filled with inviting, overstuffed furniture. It enticed everyone to exhale deeply. Like its owners, it was warm and comfortable, especially on this cold November morning. Donovan was on his own, a mission to the best sports shop, somewhere in Nebraska. It was a four-hour drive from Casper. His quest — the world's best fishing lures.

While we visited John and Sylvia, I had scheduled some private spiritual counseling sessions, from one to three hours each, depending on the client. Usually clients want to experience a deeper dimension to their lives than they have created for themselves. During these sessions, I read their subtle energies and the direction of their Spirit and provide information and insights about why painful and defeating patterns play out in their lives, and how to recognize and create healthier and more fulfilling alternatives.

Private sessions with clients are deep and intense, exploring the importance and purpose of their life here and next steps for their personal spiritual evolution. Often their structures of consciousness have them stuck and high-centered, so we employ a variety of self-discovery techniques to help them move past their pain, limiting beliefs and inappropriate behaviors that might impede their progress. Clients discover what makes them feel joyful and identify more opportunities to allow those activities into their lives. With this new information, often they experience profound spiritual breakthroughs that affect even their perceptions of everyday life.

Much of the time while I was engaged with clients, I was in an altered state of consciousness. My personality stepped aside so that I could read my clients accurately. I also tended to be chilled. Even if it was summer, my body temperature dropped as energy flowed through me.

I completed a two-hour session with my first client and was waiting for the next one to arrive. I felt odd, as if someone had turned up the thermostats on both heat and energy frequencies. I got so hot I threw open the windows and removed layers of clothing down to a thin tee shirt.

I said to myself, "I'll figure out what this is later. I'm not ill, I know that. But my energies seem to be boosted."

Halfway through the next session, the switch in my body was thrown again. The frequency amped up. Somehow, I managed to get through the meeting with my client, although I felt as if the whole room were dripping with sweat. Gratefully, when my client left, I went downstairs and noticed that Sylvia had opened all the doors to the crisp fall day. I sat down in an easy chair. "Something is happening here." I said, "I am so hot. I feel like my body is overheating."

"I know. I can't understand it. It's cool outside. In here it's like high summer. It's so hot we had to open the doors to get cross-ventilation. What's going on up there?"

"I don't know Sylvia, I can't read for my next client. Could you please call her and cancel the appointment for me? I feel like I'm going to pass out."

As Sylvia reached for the phone, I thought a bit of food might ground my fluxing energy a little. I took a few sips from a bowl of Sylvia's homemade soup, but I could get only a little down. I had no appetite.

I felt estranged from my body, more so as the energy accelerated moment by moment. I went into the living room and huddled by myself. I was curious, but not afraid even though I had never experienced anything like it before.

I prayed for guidance; "Dear Spirit of God, I know that whatever is happening is perfectly fine and I'll be okay, but I'm a little nervous. I feel like what's coming through me is bigger than I've ever been. Help me to expand my capacities and surrender into it. And let me know what I need to do to assist the process."

Sylvia came in to sit with me for a little while. I was

sweating. Beads of moisture stood out on my forehead. I said to her, "Will you just put your hands on my body and help me relax?"

"Yes, of course." She guided me upstairs to her treatment room and put on some soft music while I laid face down on her massage table. I felt as though racing waves of heat were running over my skin. Sylvia placed one hand on my lower spine and the other in the middle of my back. Her touch stabilized me so that I could assimilate whatever Spirit had in mind. She didn't try to change, fix or heal anything. I believe she became a channel, a conduit for divine cosmic force to flow through her into me.

Hot as I was, her hands felt hotter as energy pulsed through them. I muttered a repetitive litany: "I give myself to Spirit, I give myself to Spirit." Even listening to the soothing strain of Vivaldi, it was impossible for me to relax. Intensified heat and energy plunged through me.

Suddenly, I saw in my mind, clear as a movie, lifelike images, of what I perceived to be a past life. Within a split second, I saw an entire lifetime, its purpose, its usefulness and its message. Then more slides popped into my mind's eye, one lifetime after another. Like an Akashic slide show, I watched the recorded account of my soul's evolution. There was a mother and child walking down a country road, an architect of an ancient civilization, a light being, a chemist in a white lab coat, a native woman washing deer-hide clothes in a river, a beggar huddled on a city street, a condemned woman slowly walking toward a guillotine, a temple priest in Egypt. I'm not sure all of the lifetimes I saw were on this planet. I know some of the lives were lived in other dimensions. In the whole of the slide show that reeled past my mind I recognized the vibration of my own soul's journey.

Soon the slide show went dark. I was calmed by a faint-green, glowing energy flowing through my body from head to toe, lulling every cell into sweet surrender. It vibrated with iridescent light. I exhaled deeply into suspended animation. I became the space between two breaths.

Now, I was both in my body and outside of it. My eyes felt like they had expanded and I could see far beyond my normal range of vision. Multi-perceptual, I saw myself standing, a silent observer beside the table. And then I saw an amorphous, wispy, white energy begin to extract itself from my familiar, prostrate body. Gossamer filaments of energy peeled away and coalesced into a vaguely human yet diaphanous form that languidly lifted up and out of my physical body. It hovered momentarily, at a ninety degree angle as if to collect itself, then, poof! disappeared into the ethers.

I knew then with a joy as deep as forever that I was going home. Home to the limitless place my tour guides had introduced me to. Yes! The Spirit named Shari was leaving her body behind forever. As I leaped free I heard that steady magnificent hum, that overwhelming tone of love, the sound of All That Is, the sound of God, welcoming me back to my source.

As I drew further away from my body, I felt no sense of loss, grief, emptiness or fear. Somehow I knew with deep insight how the script was destined to play out. This was simply the next scene. Suddenly, as though she felt the energy shift, Sylvia removed her hands and took several steps across the room and sat down. Her eyes widened in anticipation of what was to come next.

From infinity, as though through another inter-dimensional portal, hurtled a fist-sized globe of golden light. It was the essence of a completely new spiritual entity, vibrating at a vast frequency. It radiated an unstoppable sense of purpose, as if driven to fulfill its destiny. As it approached it grew bigger and bigger until its energy filled the entire room. Its intense core blasted into the vacant, prone body at the base of the spine. The penetrating impact exploded into and filled to capacity each individual cell, one after another, millions of them. When the cellular metamorphosis and Spirit transfer were complete, the body relaxed. Shari was gone. I had arrived. Immediately, I felt suspended, swimming in a golden white ocean of peaceful infinity beyond words, in the heart of pure joy.

14

The Walk-In

I blinked my eyes open in my new life and somehow lifted my new body up to my knees and sat back. My entire field of vision was consumed by a dance of vivid light in a breathtaking spectrum I couldn't recognize. Sometimes the light danced in a grid, sometimes in swirls of tumbling color, sometimes in tiny, brilliant balls that skipped and curled and bounced on the walls of the room. I felt urged to dance with the color-music, and I moved my arms gently over my head like slender palm trees in a breeze, waving the rich sounds into my body. More than a dance, the music became a welcoming ritual, assimilating its light patterns and colors into my body to strengthen the foundation for a new energy. I heard myself speaking audibly a strange language like an articulated harmonic form of light. I understood the meaning of every word, syllable and thought. After what felt like a few minutes, the transmitted language and the ballet of light faded. My arms slowly stopped undulating and rested quietly at my sides. I saw the woman whose name I knew as Sylvia stand up and walk back to the end of the table. She was transfixed. I swung my body around to face her, yet could feel my personality still on the sidelines.

An energy presence I couldn't identify, but would come to recognize later, began speaking through me. I participated physically, looking through eyes adjusted by the new energy. A smile spread over my face. My mouth opened and energy-influenced words began to come out. Directed at Sylvia, I heard and understood them although they were spoken in an unfamiliar accent, "We are so happy to be with you. You are the first to see us. We honor and thank you for assisting in this process. The Spirit which you have identified as Shari is complete and is now departed. We are present, holding the frequency and adjusting the body while the new vibration assimilates itself. The new vibration, the new Spirit, will be called 'Juelle.' Although some will call her 'Jewel,' her name is 'Ju-elle.' She needs to know this. You will tell her all that has happened since she will not remember it right away. As we said, Shari is gone."

Sylvia gasped, "Oh my God! What's happening? Is this is real? Who's Juelle? Where did Shari go?"

The unfamiliar voice continued, "Juelle is another unique expression, a vaster aspect of the complete soul entity of which Shari was also a part. Shari has fulfilled her mission here, and has acted as a conduit for us to assist transforming this frequency. She has been preparing for this transfer. The transition to Juelle is now complete."

Sylvia responded under her breath, "Something really *happened* didn't it? I'm not imagining things. You're a different person."

The voice speaking through me explained, "Juelle

will be very confused. It will take several months for the new energy to be completely adjusted. Although the adjustment will be a bit difficult for her, everything will be fine. This is her next step. Again, we wish to thank you for your participation."

I could feel this benevolent energy step away and linger at the sidelines while my personality emerged back to the surface. I became fully conscious, even though I vaguely sensed the energy supporting me like a guardian angel. My own voice returned, "Sylvia, what just happened?"

Moved to tears, unable to explain, she said, "I'm not sure … but this is what I saw." Patiently, she described what had happened in the room during the last two hours. "I ran my hands down your spine. When I reached somewhere around your waist, in my mind's eye I saw a greenish light come through my arms and into your back. I felt its power. Nothing like this has ever happened to me before. You raised up effortlessly. I removed my hands and stood back in awe as you got to your knees. Your back looked spineless, like a jellyfish, and your arms moved fluidly along with your body, in a somehow sacred, almost Oriental-looking dance, but it was like nothing I have ever seen before. I moved to the chair, sat down and watched. I was so filled with emotion that tears dropped into my hands."

I corroborated the details she recounted through my own experience of them. It felt like putting together a three-dimensional puzzle, pieces from Shari, from Sylvia and from another energy source I couldn't even identify. The paradox tumbled through my consciousness and left me with an overwhelming sense of disbelief. "Can this be true?" And yet knowing all the while that it was. Shari was indeed gone. I felt different in a profound way, but I was extremely disoriented. I asked Sylvia, "What do I do now?"

I suddenly felt very upset, confused and shaken to the core.

Sylvia continued, "When I first heard that first unusual, accented voice I thought, 'I don't believe this! You're making this up.' But I realized that you couldn't have contrived it. I panicked, 'How am I going to remember all of this? Why pick *me?'* Although I don't understand all of it, I know you're different. And you're going to have to be patient with yourself. From what they said, you're brand new in Shari's body. She's gone. She won't be back. And your name is 'Juelle.' I know, this sounds crazy to me too! The idea of a new Spirit seems farfetched, yet I'm convinced it's true. I don't understand why it happened, but it did." She repeated what the energy source spoke through me.

I sat stock still, trying to assimilate the mystery.

She consoled me, "Let's just sit here for a minute and we'll go downstairs when you're ready. God, what's John going to say?" We sat together for fifteen minutes while my mind reeled. I could only utter grunts of disbelief.

Finally, we went downstairs into the kitchen where John sat reading the paper. He looked up at me, "What's happened? You don't look quite yourself."

Sylvia and I sat down at the kitchen table alongside him. She described as carefully as possible the details that she could remember about the experience.

John kept eyeing me, "Where did Shari go?"

I answered, "I don't know. I'm so confused. At this moment, I can't tell you that. All I can say is that she is gone. And I am Juelle. I'm not clear about what this means, but I know I'm not who I was when I came into this house." I searched to find words that would express my frustration, but I kept hitting a wall of confusion.

I looked around the room, taking inventory of objects that had been so familiar to me only hours before, trying to make sense of a strange new world. I knew that I knew what things were, but I had to search through Shari's memory to remind myself, "Oh yes ... books. Oh yes ... chair ... television." I noticed my hands on the top of the table. I could feel my fingers, wrists and arms, "Oh these are attached. It's an entire unit."

Sylvia asked me if I wanted a bowl of soup. "Soup ... food ... hungry. Am I? Yes! Soup. Nice and warm." I remained intrigued by my hands. They automatically knew how to hold the spoon, scoop the food, and bring it to my mouth.

Sounds were amplified much louder than usual. I could see thoughts forming into words in Sylvia and John's minds long before they came out. Even their thoughts seemed loud. When the words finally emerged, they reverberated, as if echoing from the walls of a deep canyon. Laughter was almost unbearable to me because of its intensity and elevated decibel level.

All of a sudden Donovan's face flashed into my mind. I panicked, "Oh my God! He is Shari's husband! He went away for the day and he's going to come home to an entirely different person, one whom he calls 'wife.'" I could feel the softness in Shari's heart, my heart, for the man Donovan. There was no question that I would be able to accept and love him too.

But I felt apprehensive. Because I felt so strange in my body, I also felt that I must look contorted, as if I had stretched my skin to get into it. I was afraid of what Donovan would think when he saw me, and doubly concerned about what he would think when he found out that I wasn't Shari. Would he like me? Would he want to be with me? I grabbed Sylvia's arm and gushed, "Donovan! What's he going to think when he gets back? You've got to help me explain this to him!"

Calmer than I had expected, Sylvia consoled me, "Everything will be fine. Donovan is so intuitive that he may already be picking up that something's happened to you. Maybe that's why he went away for the day. Why don't you take a warm bath and try to relax? It'll make you feel better."

She walked me into the bathroom and drew my bath. I sank into the warm water up to my chin. My mind raced, searching through all the records in Shari's reference library, to find any bits of information to help explain this mystery. I sighed, either I was going crazy, which deep in my heart I knew was not true, or I was going to have to accept the remarkable idea that I was Juelle, a new entity.

I glanced down at my body through the water, studying the human package in which I found myself. Drawing my fingers up my arm, I neither delighted in it nor was put off by it, simply curious, analyzing the equipment I had to work with. I needed to get used to the form, to being inside of it, to understand how it moved. It was all so strange, breathing inside a body, looking out through it and sensing from so few sources of input. Taking the bath indeed helped me feel more comfortable.

I had to re-familiarize myself with my surroundings. This was Wyoming. This was Sylvia and John's house. I'd slept in this bedroom for two nights. The clothes on the chair were my clothes. Among them I found some comfortable things to put on, pink sweat pants and a matching sweatshirt.

I didn't want to be alone for long. Sylvia and John were my link to this new world and I wanted to stay close to them. I joined them again at the kitchen table. Sylvia asked, "How is your name spelled?" She brought a pencil and a pad to the table and handed them to me. We scribbled one possibility after another until we found the one that seemed to match my energy vibration: "J-u-e-l-l-e." I took the piece of paper into the bedroom and put it on the dresser, careful not to lose my name or the correct spelling of it.

Just then, through the window, I saw Donovan pull in the driveway. My stomach felt nervous and queasy. I held my breath. What was I going to say, "Hi! meet your new wife. A funny thing happened on the way to work today?"

Donovan walked in the door, loaded with packages. He headed straight to the bedroom without speaking to anyone. A moment later he came into the kitchen carrying the piece of paper with the various spellings of my name. He held it in his hand, looked directly at me, and with a knowing smile said, "You've changed, haven't you? You're different. Shari's not here is she?"

I was overcome with relief and whispered under my breath, "Thank you, Spirit."

It was clear to me immediately that Donovan's own spiritual strength influenced his equanimity in the face of such an enigmatic event as I posed. His infinite trust translated into a unwavering confidence that regardless of the external circumstances, all was truly well. He sat down with us at the table. "What happened here today?" he asked.

Sylvia and John recounted the whole story in as much detail as possible. Donovan reached over and took my hand, "Shall we go have a talk?"

We excused ourselves to the bedroom and sat, face to face on the bed. I told him everything I could remember about what happened that afternoon. He listened matter-of-factly. I kept watching him for a glimmer of a negative reaction. He didn't flinch. I said, "For some reason, and I'm not sure why, I was so thankful that you weren't here. I was afraid that I would look strange or grotesque to you. But now, I'm really thankful that you're back. I have no idea what any of this means or how it will influence our lives."

Donovan put his arms around me, "We both know that only the highest possibility happens in our lives. Whatever this is, it's perfectly directed by your Spirit and by mine. So here we go, we'll see where *this* adventure takes us. And we'll explore it together."

15

The
Disorientation

I slept fitfully during most of the drive back to Montana. I dozed, then awoke thinking, "My life's the same, it was just a dream." Suddenly, a new thought interjected itself, "No it isn't, and I wasn't dreaming. What happened was real."

I knew it was real when I remembered the soothing bath at Sylvia's. That was the first time I had seen my new body naked. I took off the clothes I was wearing, a sweatshirt that hung to my knees, a pair of tight bluejeans and tennis shoes. When I removed the pink bra and panties, I was startled by all the flesh I saw. My breasts stood up the way they were supposed to, and my blonde hair was thick and naturally wavy. I sensed, however, that Shari disapproved of the distribution of flesh on this body. The words "too fat" came into my head.

I thought about this observation for a moment, and decided that Shari was wrong. My new body was too skinny. I was surprised by the thought. I, me, Juelle, had stated a clear preference. I had asserted an opinion about the body I'd inherited. For some reason, I was pleased that I had spoken my preference. It was a step forward toward establishing my own personality.

Many changes began to happen to me as I settled into my new identity. I became convinced that, though I had no memory of my previous life before I came into Shari's body, I was indeed a visitor, a newcomer who had been given a flesh-and-blood body in which to reside. Since I was thinking with Shari's mind but with my personality superimposed, it was natural I should be confused. It was at that moment that Shari's memories of her daughter, Christian, rushed over me. In many respects I was as helpless as the infant Christian had been. But Christian had progressed slowly from a wriggling baby, a *tabula rasa,* a book without words written in it, to crawling, walking, and talking, taking years to assimilate and respond to her environment. She had examined her fingers and toes, grown hair and teeth, and changed the color of her eyes — all on a predetermined time table.

I, on the other hand, had been plunged into a mature body, replacing an embodied Spirit, who left behind 40 years of memories, food and clothing preferences, favored music, an intellectual and physical history of doubts and convictions, aches and pains, hopes and dreams, tastes and biases. As a matter of fact, one of the first things I replaced was Shari's shade of lipstick. It was too dark. I decided I liked a lighter, more pastel shade. I'd been furnished with a worldly body that knew, without prompting, what to do with a toothbrush, television and toaster.

Yet I had to give myself time to understand the assimilation process I was bound to undertake. Each day I would face new problems, new challenges. I'd have to call on the wisdom Shari left behind and test it against my own preferences as they became firmly established.

My Spirit, my personality, began to penetrate Shari's body deep into every cell and fiber, as it had when the dramatic transformation took place. As a result, on a conscious level, I began to absorb Shari's cellular memories. This was like, I thought, soaking the pores of my new skin with the flavor of my own soul. I considered that analogy and was not satisfied with it, but it was the best I could do at the time.

Walking through the front door of Shari's house was another step into someone else's life. All the things that belonged to Shari were now mine. I inherited an entire life intact. It wasn't my life and yet it was. I walked into my office, "What do I do here? Oh yes, I make calls and work here." Boxes were strewn all over the floor, "That's right, we're packing. We're moving to Washington!"

Suddenly, Christian flashed into my mind. I felt queasy about facing her. What if she rejected me? What if I couldn't mother her in the way that she had been used to? How could I explain this so that she would understand? Buying myself some time, I phoned her. Concerned that I wouldn't be able to interact with her in the familiar way, I simply offered, "Christian, something incredible and very life-changing has happened to me. I'm still sorting it out. It isn't anything to be afraid of. It's a wonderful thing. I want to see you in person to tell you about it. We're leaving for Washington for a week to find a place to live. We'll stop by on the way back and talk about it with you then."

The events of that day at Sylvia's looped around and around in my mind. I ping-ponged around inside the immense paradox. I am Shari, Shari is me and yet I am not Shari and Shari is not me. I got lost in it again. I truly didn't understand what had happened. I was afraid despite all the assurances and the bravado I had mustered up.

Donovan offered to help me through my panic, but he couldn't truly realize the depth and the scope of the experience. I phoned my close friend, Kathleen, and tried to explain my new identity and all the sensations associated with it. If anyone could understand she could. She and Shari often talked about the mysteries of the invisible realms. I tried to find words to describe what had happened, but when I tried to put the events into words, they sounded ridiculous. Because she knew others who had experienced similar radical shifts in consciousness, she consoled me as best she could, "Congratulations! A wonderful thing has happened to you. We can talk about it more next week when you and Donovan come to Washington. Don't worry, it'll make sense to you soon enough."

I sighed and decided to examine the clothes and personal effects I inherited from Shari. Maybe I could find some sanity in them. The clothes hanging in her closet depressed me. A row of colorless dresses, drab blues, browns, mauves, grays. And business suits. How dreadful!

In a chest of drawers, I found blue jeans, several pairs. They were clinging and tight, but I decided to force myself to like them. I stuck my legs into the denim tubes and yanked them up. When I jerked the crotch into place and snapped the metal fastener shut, I almost choked. I felt nauseous. My skin cringed. The pants gripped me tightly, pulling at my skin, restricting my movements.

I couldn't stand them. Frantically, I pulled them off and kicked them away. I tripped myself and fell on my knees, frustrated and crying. I hated those things. I'd never wear them. Never!

I found some loose cotton pants with balloon-like

legs and a floppy sweater. They were comfortable and I wore them until I was sure Donovan was sick of the sight of them.

It was just a couple of days after the transformation when Donovan reminded me that we needed to shop for food. A picture came into my mind of a grocery store with aisles of selections, rows of cans, colored shapes of fruits and vegetables, and the smell of bread wafting from the bakery section. I looked forward to the adventure until we actually walked into the supermarket. Then I panicked.

All the bustling people frightened me, and I balked when I looked at the mounds of dead squash, and lifeless lettuce, carrots and dirty potatoes that had been dug out of the ground.

My shopping trips were like breathless marathons. I'd whisk around the grocery store with a list of things to get, racing against the "crowded" feeling that clutched at me. I never completed my list. I must have looked like a Jack rabbit, hopping nervously from the meat counter to the bakery section, grabbing a carton of milk and throwing apples and tomatoes into plastic bags. My movements were frenzied and awkward, like someone being chased.

Waiting in line at the checkout stand was a nightmare. I learned to keep my choices under 10 items so I could rush through the express line. The grocery checker must have thought I was crazy when I rushed up and dropped the few items I'd chosen on the counter in front of him. I felt nauseous, hemmed in, flustered and miserable. When he gave me my change, I didn't even glance at it, I just jammed it in my purse, grabbed my bag and ran.

After that experience, I looked more closely in the kitchen for some kind of a drink that would contain nutrients my new body needed. Of course, there wasn't anything.

The name of a special drink came into my head, and I asked Donovan if we had any "Liquid Light!" He looked at me quizzically, then said, "I've never heard of that."

I took his word that the concoction wasn't made on this planet. It was strange that I knew the name for the drink, but had no memory of what it looked like, or how it tasted.

I was confused by the constant references to sexuality repeated in every aspect of human life. I assumed that sexual union was a natural expression of human relationships, as inevitable as any other physical experience. The notion contradicted my inner knowing that I came from a place inhabited by all-loving androgynous beings where sex isn't even an issue.

Patient with me, Donovan soon took over the grocery shopping because invariably I'd forget something. I was relieved and grateful. During the weeks following the transformation, the meals we ate in the house were never complete. I'd always forget something, or offer odd combinations such as pasta and potatoes. Donovan didn't complain much, but I caught him studying me with a puzzled look on his face, or I'd hear him sigh with frustration when he searched the empty fridge. It must have been difficult for him living with a woman who bore every resemblance to his wife, but who acted like a bewildered foreigner.

My own emerging personality became more apparent when I discovered that mall shopping was impossible for me — all the clothes looked the same. If the feeling that the walls were closing in was pronounced in the grocery store, it became overwhelming at a big shopping mall. I fled, unable to force myself to window shop or pick through the items like the other shoppers. I couldn't understand how they tolerated being jostled, delayed in lines, offered things that looked funny or out of place or didn't fit. I couldn't fathom why negligent clerks stood around gazing into space while I tried to get their attention.

I finally found a women's boutique away from the mall which carried what Donovan termed "exotic" clothes. That was how he described the clothes I bought: colorful cotton pants, aqua, white and lavender blouses, a glittering long shirt over gold lamé leggings and silver and gold shoes. When he saw I was happy with my choices, he praised my selection.

One day I edged open the door to Shari's meditation room. The comfortable chaise lounge invited me to rest. I wrapped one of Grandma's quilts up to my chin and sank into the chair. I cried and cried, surrendering my anguish. "My dear Spirit, help me." I knew that I wasn't losing my mind because I could clearly identify Shari's entire life in sharp relief and knew that I had to claim it as my own, but I had so many questions, "Do I claim all of it? Only parts of it? What about *my* life? What *is* mine? Who am I? Any memory of my 'self' was veiled to me. I couldn't access where I came from or why. But I *saw* myself come in ... didn't I? Yes, I'm *sure* of it."

I felt a desperate determination. "I'm moving to Washington. I have people in my life to take care of. I can't allow myself to sink." Suddenly I recognized a familiar energy that buoyed me up. It was the same supportive strength that had surrounded me during my transformation experience. I could feel its strong presence all around me, and inside me at the same time. Simultaneously, I felt, heard and sensed it reassure me, "All is well. Just take the next step, and the next one, and the next one. You will soon come to understand all of this."

The next day we left for Washington. Donovan drove the pickup, towing the aluminum fishing boat, while I followed him in the car. It was an unusual sensation to be behind the wheel of a car. I knew what to do, but I felt unsure of myself, so I relied on Shari's driving expertise, her experienced reactions to common road hazards. She had become an intrepid driver, having driven many hours across the mountainous Montana landscape. Still, I felt spacey, not really in my body. "I'll just follow the back of Donovan's boat. It'll be fine. These two days of driving will be very useful. I'll have plenty of time to think about what's happened and the energy will have a chance to assimilate. I'll get more insights."

We'd been driving for about five hours. I was getting used to my new internal and external conditions and the density of my new dimension. I even managed to smile now and then when everyday events seemed humorous to me. For instance, it was pouring rain as we reached the Idaho border. Donovan pulled off to the side of the road. I carefully followed him onto the shoulder. He got out of the truck and walked back to the car. I looked up at him through the rain-streaked window. He stood there in the pouring rain looking at me expectantly.

I thought, "Why is he standing there? He can come inside easily, just 'phase' through the door." I waited for him while he stood there, rain dripping off the end of his nose, for several seconds. Finally, he knocked hard on the window and spoke loudly, forming his words with exaggerated facial expressions, "Roll-down-the-window!"

"Oh! … Sorry!"

"What did you think I was *doing* out here?"

"I thought you'd just come in here. I *wondered* what was taking you so long."

He threw his head back and laughed. Water dripped from his drenched blond head. "It's lunch time. Are you hungry?"

"I guess."

He smiled, "Okay, we'll pull over when we get into Idaho."

"Okay, fine."

Tittering, he rolled his eyes and shrugged his shoulders. I got the message. I was in third-dimensional training.

There were moments when I felt enthusiastic about finding a new home and moving to Washington. But there were many more moments when I simply stepped through the paces with no emotional response, wondering what all the hoopla was about. Finally, I got myself into the excitement of the relocation mood. "It will be fun. I've never lived in Washington before, or lived *here* before, for that matter." As I daydreamed through Shari's bank of memories, visual reminders flooded my mind with pleasant past events. I became attached to the idea of buying an old farm house with a barn. "We could fix it up and put a few horses in the pasture."

Staying with Kathleen and Robert for the week was a blessing. Kathleen actually knew people who had gone through radical shifts, and Robert came from Hollywood where people constantly change their names, as I had done. So they both would understand me. Feeling accepted and honored helped smooth out my daily bouts of confusion. The evening we arrived, Kathleen poured me a cup of herbal tea and gently probed, "How're you doing? Do you really understand what happened that night? You know, this sounds like a 'walk-in' experience."

I let the warm tea vapors envelope my face as I thoughtfully responded, "I've been using familiar phrases to describe Shari's Spirit leaving and my Spirit coming in like 'energy exchange,' 'energy rotation,' and 'the replacement,' every label but 'walk-in.' Shari's past tells me that she was aware of the concept through readings she'd done, and that she even knew a few people who call themselves 'walk-ins,' but I'm just not sure if that's what happened to me."

Kathleen explained, "My understanding of the walk-in phenomenon is that it often occurs during near-death experiences. In a serious illness or accident, a Spirit can gracefully exit this plane and its body becomes available for another Spirit to enter."

I took a sip of tea. "It might be a common scenario, but it wasn't true in my case. Shari was neither sick, nor did she have an accident."

Kathleen refreshed her own cup of tea, set the pot on the table, and continued, "Another commonly-known variation is that a Spirit doesn't have the emotional resources to complete its mission. It may be too emotionally exhausted to go on and may even feel like committing suicide, so another Spirit can take up where it leaves off. Either way, it's always done by agreement between both Spirits at a soul level and according to the divine plan for each one."

Kathleen's description of these possibilities only heightened my confusion because I didn't experience either one. I said, "Soul-weariness was clearly not the case for Shari. Her life was full and enriched. She'd found a wonderful mate and a livelihood that suited her."

Sensing my frustration, Kathleen offered another possibility, "Well, don't you think this gives us another model? Maybe it doesn't have to happen because of physical pain and trauma, or even weariness of the soul. Maybe the reason Shari departed is just this simple: *her purpose for this lifetime was complete.* Or perhaps she had a new assignment and reached the stage in her spiritual growth where she was ready for it."

I felt relieved. Maybe there *was* a logical way to explain what had happened. The conversation with Kathleen helped me acknowledge to a greater degree that my replacement of Shari was according to a divine plan whose ultimate purpose I would learn about when I was ready for it. Over the next few months, as I remained open to the possibility that I was a walk-in, more information and insights were made clear to me.

In the meantime, Donovan and I poured over the multiple listing service book and selected three properties for the real estate agent to show us. She made appointments for us to see them all in one afternoon. We drove by the first two and could almost tell from the street that we weren't interested in looking any closer.

We turned into the long driveway of the third property, barely making out the roof line above the stand of trees when Donovan exclaimed, "This is it! This is the place! We're buying it!"

As disoriented as I was, I followed Donovan's lead on most things. But this just didn't make sense to me. We couldn't even see the house yet. As we approached it, I tried to help him understand that this was all wrong, "What do you mean? This is a modern house! Look, there's no barn here. There's no horse pasture. There's no hundred-year-old farm house. How can you say 'This is it!'?"

As we pulled into the driveway, Donovan sprang out of the agent's car and bounded around the house, claiming his territory, "This is it! I just *know* it!"

In an apologetic tone I said to the realtor, "I really don't think this is it." I was sure that I wasn't supposed to have a house like this; it was contemporary with clean lines.

Donovan beamed. Every room enchanted him, especially the living room with floor-to-ceiling windows and a wrap-around vista of the valley and Mount Rainier. He could envision the unfinished basement as a cozy den with thick carpeting and a wood stove. He had clearly found his home.

Sensing his glee, the realtor asked, "Well, shall we write an offer now?"

My throat clinched shut. "What? Right now?" I turned to Donovan, "Do you *really* think this is our house?"

"Yes! This is our house!"

"But I don't like it."

"What's not to like? Five acres? Trees? Beautiful landscaping? On top of a hill? A dynamite view? Five bedrooms? A hot tub? Windows everywhere? What's not to like?"

I could only explain, "Uh. ... Uh. ... I thought it was supposed to be a *farm.*"

He reminded me, "We already *lived* on a farm. Maybe there's something else for us to try this time." Clearly there was a glitch in my computer, so I acquiesced. We wrote an offer that afternoon. The next day we made all the arrangements for a loan. It was done. That easy.

We left the truck and the fishing boat with Kathleen and Robert in Washington and drove back to Montana together in the car. I was distracted, wondering if the full impact of my "experience" had hit me yet. "'Experience,' hmmmm. Should I *really* start calling it 'walk-in'? ... Yes."

The long drive gave me time to reflect on the new me and this new adventure. I was struck by the divine timing of it all. "I am a brand new identity. I have a new name. Soon I'll live in a new place where no one knows Shari. They will only know me as 'Juelle.' There won't be any history to keep track of, or any projections of my expected behavior. What a blessing to be given the opportunity to create it all anew."

We stopped in Bozeman, Montana to see Christian. I had butterflies in my stomach. I was both anxious to see her and nervous about how she would react to me. By this time, Christian was used to her mom and dad not living a "traditional" life. By nature, she was more conventional, perhaps as a natural response to our living an "alternative lifestyle," as she called it, making seemingly capricious decisions like moving to Costa Rica, and imbuing day-to-day events with the sense of the mystical.

My daughter Christian was a beautiful 19-year old college sophomore with dark brown, wavy hair and big brown eyes. She always looked like she stepped out of a bandbox, perfectly groomed, wearing the latest styles. At 5 feet 8 inches tall, she was very athletic, a runner and a mountain biker. Christian was just coming into her own, finding her way in the world.

After the initial hugs, greetings and chit-chat, I got right to the point. I told her the story of what happened that night at Sylvia and John's less than two weeks earlier. I explained to her, to the best of my ability, my memories of it, my responses to it, and its possible impact on our lives. "I'm still in a whirl trying to understand it."

As I spoke, her big brown eyes widened. I tried to gauge her response. "Is she following this? Does she think her mother has flipped her lid? Is she frightened?"

After a thoughtful moment, Christian let out a huge sigh. "Oh, Mom, I am so relieved. For the last month, I kept having a sensation that I was losing my mother. So I was even more petrified when you called and said that something 'life-changing' had happened. I can't tell you how relieved I am to know that I haven't lost you."

There in her words was evidence of the link between kindred souls, the silent telepathy that passes mysteriously between people when the vibrational tone of one or the other changes. I was grateful for her sensitivity. Christian had actually perceived that her mother's Spirit was preparing to leave and had departed. I loved this girl. Although I wasn't sure how to mother her, I was convinced that I wanted to play that part. "In a sense, you *have* lost the mother you knew," I said. "I don't know exactly what our relationship is going to be like, but I *do* know one thing, I love you. I want to be your mother. I am your mother. I may not be the mother you're used to or even the mother you want, but we'll have to see how it turns out. The bottom line is, I want to be in your life."

We embraced one another, each of us sighing in relief, "Thank God!" Christian turned to Donovan, "Dad, how do *you* feel about all this?"

"Well, it sure is interesting. Everything's different, but I'm fine with it. I love your mom. We're in this together. Neither one of us completely understands what's happened. But once we're moved and the dust settles we'll be able to see what this really is."

The next few weeks in Montana were devoted to tying up the loose ends and preparing for our move. I was still making major adjustments in my physical body and in the physical world, reminding myself how things were done here. I felt the presence, strongly at moments, of that guardian angel energy, differentiated and yet inexplicably part of me. It came forward in my most critical moments, at times of desperate confusion and dark despair. I sensed the presence, whispering words of support and guidance into my mind, reaffirming that everything was fine, "You are a spark of the Divine with a unique part to play. This is not a mistake, it is not just an accident. This mission is for purposeful good and you will come to understand it all."

I drew a blank on the simplest things. We planned a huge garage sale to jettison unnecessary items: floral samples, light fixtures, garden tools and duplicate kitchen items. I had three spatulas, a large pancake flipper with a painted green handle and a fringe of rust around its aluminum scraper, a tiny one with white paint scuffing off its handle, and a black plastic one, intended for Teflon pans, which had gouges in it where the plastic melted against hot pans. I picked them up and studied them, "Do I want these? Do I even *like* them? Will they be useful?"

Donovan noticed that I was evaluating all of them and asked, "Are you keeping those three old spatulas?"

The question threw me. "I don't know ... Shouldn't we?"

He chuckled, "Living with you is like living with someone who's got amnesia."

"Why?"

"I got used to Shari's responses. There's about a three-second delay in how you react. And I'm never quite sure *how* you're going to respond when you *do*."

Puzzled, I asked, "What do you mean?"

"For instance, Shari was tactful and careful when offering advice; you don't seem to mince words. Shari had a lot of patience; you seem to have none. Shari was a semi-strict vegetarian and loved children and rock and roll music. You eat meat, don't seem to care much about children, and can't stand rock and roll. Sometimes it's confusing to live with someone who's had an overnight personality change."

I smiled, "Oh ... yeah, you're right. But the truth is I'm still exploring my responses myself, what I like and what I want. Until I really *do* know what I want, I'll just pack all three of these spatulas and sort them out later." Exasperated, I tossed them all into a Washington-bound carton.

My outer world reflected my inner world. All of Shari's memories were accessible to me, the entire storehouse of them, both the pictures and the emotions associated with them. It all seemed so overwhelming. Because I couldn't discern their relative importance in my life I'd have to sort through all the memories individually at a later time. How was I going to do that? How many recollections makeup 40 years of a lifetime? That's what I had inherited.

I packed Shari's meditation room last. It was obvious that stepping into this sacred space was intended to elevate the God consciousness. Devotional items sat on a low cedar chest alter covered with a white lacy cloth: pictures of spiritual masters, peach, pink and purple candles, rocks and feathers, souvenirs of hikes in the woods and mountains. While I was packing the room, I ran across Shari's journals. In a meditative state, she was inspired to write about her perspectives on love, raising a child, living in Costa Rica, her pilgrimage to India and the mysteries of life.

In a big yellow spiral notebook she had written a detailed description of her next home, "… as if the house has no walls because expansive windows showcase the outdoors; landscaped grounds with deva-filled gardens; a house so high on a hill it seems to hover in the air." Of all the crazy things, she added some details like, "a wood stove and a hot tub for Donovan." I took a deep breath. Shari had foreseen and described in detail the actual house Donovan and I had bought. The house even offered some bonuses, *two* wood stoves, one in the living room upstairs and one in the downstairs den, and *two* hot tubs, one outside on the deck and the other a sunken Jacuzzi in the master bathroom.

Somehow I absolutely knew that this was not the kind of house that Shari would have preferred. I felt as though she had written her vision down for me, as though some part of her had known that our new home would be the most energetically supportive environment for Juelle. It was a supreme confirmation that I was taken care of.

I ran through the house as fast as I could to show Donovan, who was packing tools in the garage. I pointed to the yellow cover of the notebook. "Donovan, have you ever seen this notebook?"

"No. What is it?"

"It's Shari's meditation journal. Listen to this. ..." I read him the entire vision. "Isn't this just magnificent? Thank you for sticking to your guns when I questioned your impulse to buy this house."

He nodded his head thoughtfully, "What's the date on that?"

"Two months before we found the new house in Washington. Before I walked in."

16

The
Integration

We had accumulated more "stuff" than we realized, living for six years in Montana, so we treated ourselves to a "real" move. We boxed everything up and hired professional movers to pack up the van and meet us in Washington four days later. We stayed with Kathleen and Robert while we awaited the van. The new house was spotless. There was nothing to do except move in. When the movers arrived, I stood at the door, directing men with boxes to the appropriate places throughout the house.

For some reason, we felt driven to put our house in order as if we had some important work to do, but we had no idea what the work was. We unpacked with great urgency, as though the timing were critical. I woke up at 4 a.m. to unpack the office boxes while Donovan went downstairs to assemble the workshop. In the old house, devotional items were concentrated in the meditation room. In this house, I spread them everywhere. The whole house became a sacred space, just as my whole life had become a meditation. In a matter of four days, every picture was hung and every book found a spot on the shelves. We sank into this house as if it were an easy chair which we wanted to park ourselves in forever. Kathleen was astounded. "It looks like you've lived here for years!" she said.

After the energy burst of scurrying around to put the house together, Donovan and I looked at one another, proverbially drumming our fingers, waiting to see what would present itself, waiting for the other shoe to drop. We asked ourselves, "What's next? Now what?" We had uprooted ourselves, changed our lives and moved to a place where we knew no one except for Kathleen and Robert who helped us expand our social orbit by introducing us to a few friends they had made in the area. But there was no new business on the horizon or spiritual workshops scheduled.

As the holidays approached, we looked forward to having Christian home with us. We wanted her to see our new house and meet our friends. Since they would all be with us for Christmas dinner, I wanted everything to be perfect for them. Too perfect, I thought. Like an involuntary reflex, I was worried about whether the turkey would be done on time and whether the Christmas tree and trimmings would be just right. I turned these disaster fantasies over and over in my head, analyzing them from every direction. I was actually nervous, as though something vital were at stake. "People will think I don't have it all together. What if they don't like what I've done?"

I also had an involuntary response to play the mother role. The truth was that I didn't feel much like either a mother or a wife, yet both of those parts were there to play. Although I spoke the parts, I didn't feel that they honestly reflected who I was. Intense confusion set in because I truly loved Christian and wanted to be her mother and I truly loved Donovan and wanted to be his wife. I also loved my friends. I wanted to honor all of them with a nice meal and a perfect holiday celebration. But something felt terribly amiss.

Even though all of our guests loved the house and enjoyed the meal, I sat at the dinner table with them wearing a plastic smile, noticing that some part of me felt detached. Social interaction, celebrating traditions, chit-chat and stories about the past seemed irrelevant. I couldn't find any place to participate. Yet I loved all these people. I honored that we had stories to tell together, but I felt very alone as if I were in a distant world, trying desperately to be connected to this one. I attempted to formulate words to describe my feelings. In their desire to help, friends psychoanalyzed me, interpreting my feelings based on typical human behavior. "Be patient, you've experienced some sort of spiritual change and have moved halfway across the country. That's enough to disorient most people." But I didn't buy it. These insecure feelings went deeper than that.

Everyone seemed so comfortable with their own lives. They laughed. They lived day to day, content with what they were doing. They loved telling stories of their lives, identifying who they were today based upon the stories of the past. It didn't make sense to me. I wanted to ask, "So who are you *now?* What's important to you *now?"* Of course, I never asked; it seemed so inappropriate. I struggled to find a reference point and instead felt an intense yearning to go home, but couldn't remember where "home" was. I just knew that it wasn't here. Home wasn't anything like this at all.

Somehow, I managed to get through the holidays. All the fanfare was over and Christian went back to school. Distractions gone, I had to deal with my discomfort. I felt like a stranger in a strange land. Nothing made sense to me. A wave of emotion would bowl me over, touching off an automatic response over which I had no control. I felt like a character in someone else's play.

Negotiating through daily life seemed foreign to me, like waking up one day with one leg and one eye missing. Yet I perceived myself as whole, with all my limbs and both eyes intact. The essence of me didn't feel desperate, afraid or inferior and yet these emotions were playing out in me. For instance, one night we had invited a few friends over for dinner. I went to the garage to get some more soda while Donovan served drinks to our guests in the kitchen. He noticed that the kitchen floor was wet. When he opened the cabinet under the kitchen sink, water gushed out like a river. He yelled to me at the top of his lungs, "Juelle, get in here! There's water running everywhere!"

A shock wave shot through my body! I was galvanized by his voice. Overcome with panic and terror, I grabbed a bucket and rags, and like a whirling dervish, rushed to the scene as fast as I could to avert the impending doom. This felt like a life-threatening situation. I could be in possible physical harm. Almost hysterical, I crawled under the sink and turned off the spigot. I tried to make everyone feel better. "It's gonna' be okay. It'll be alright." With a flurry of activity, I cleaned up the mess. Everyone took three steps backward and stared at me, including Donovan.

Throughout the rest of the evening I reverberated from my fear of Donovan's voice. I kept searching for a reasonable explanation to my frenzied reaction to his excitement that flipped a switch in me somewhere. I couldn't recover from the fright I felt. I bobbed my head, smiling at our guests, trying to engage in their conversation, all the while searching through Shari's memory. "Why on Earth would a raised voice trigger such panic and terror in me? My life is not in peril here! Why did I react like that?"

Later that night, after our friends had gone home, I told Donovan how I was feeling. "When you yelled 'Water!' why didn't I say to you, 'Well, clean it up!'? Why did I come running like a banshee to mop up the mess? Why did I have to make everything right and do all of the work, as if to protect myself in order to survive?"

Donovan explained, "I wasn't yelling at you. I just saw the water and yelled for help! I wasn't yelling at you at all."

"I know. You were just excited. But I'm noticing my responses. And they're very uncomfortable."

This was the invitation Donovan needed to be frank with me. "I'm not used to such exaggerated reactions. What's the matter?"

"It's hard to explain, but I feel like I'm driven to play out an old story that isn't even mine. And it's one story right after another just waiting to be expressed."

"Your responses are uncomfortable for me too. I feel so helpless. What can I do to help you get through this?"

"Just realize that this is something I've got to do. Don't worry about me, I'm okay. I just have to express these emotions as quickly as they come up. Please don't think that anything is wrong with me that has to be fixed. Just love me and support me. I'll let you know if there's anything specific you can do in the moment. In the meantime, I want you to know how much I care about you and how much I appreciate the fact that you're willing to walk through this with me."

"I just wonder sometimes how much longer this process is going to take."

"So do I. I just know that it's a natural part of my being here. I have no choice but to work with the memories I inherited from Shari. They feel like they're lodged in my cells, just sitting there waiting to be activated. All it takes is a loud voice, and the emotion rolls over me again."

Donovan seemed puzzled, "I thought you already had made peace with all this stuff."

I shook my head. "I'm not sure I'll ever be able to overcome Shari's instinctive responses to abuse. Remember, we talked about it lots of times. Whenever she was threatened, as a child, as a woman in an abusive relationship, she was terrified. She answered violence with numb acquiescence. She rushed to please — just like I did in the kitchen — to avoid punishment. A loud voice always set her off, warning her of inevitable harm. I've inherited her responses to intimidation. A loud voice was like a bell to her, ringing in all her defensive behavior."

Donovan nodded his head in understanding. "I'm sorry I frightened you."

"It wasn't you who frightened me. It was my response to Shari's conditioning."

I understood that memories of emotional impact in this and other lifetimes are stored in the subconscious mind and very subtly emerge in consciousness as beliefs about how we see the world and our place in it. We then build behavior patterns around these beliefs. My conscious mind may say, "It's a safe world," and know that it is true, while my subconscious program contradicts, "No it isn't! Look what happened when you were five or twenty-one! Beware! Be afraid!" That subconscious memory carries a potent emotional charge that can supersede the rational thinking mind. Shari's reactions and behaviors were in response to her early conditioning and had nothing to do with my current reality. Yet I was she, and her reality, old and new, belonged to me.

So, my responses to her old script were dramatic and inappropriate. I had to learn to overcome Shari's shadow emotions when fear triggered bad recollections in me. For the next four months I fought to overcome her dysfunctional behavior patterns. Once I slipped into one there was no turning back. It was like emotional quicksand sucking me under. I let myself fill up with whatever emotion accompanied the behavior — anger, fear, sadness, until it was expressed. For example, one day I stood at the living room window looking out at the trees, happy and grateful to be living in such a beautiful place. The next minute, a wave of sadness swept over me and I dropped onto the sofa in a puddle of tears.

Donovan came into the room, "What's the matter, Honey?"

"I don't know. I can't find a reason right now. I just feel sad."

He sat down beside me and wrapped his arms around me. He just held me, neither afraid or impatient. He freely offered tolerance and understanding because by this time he knew that I was dealing with vestiges of Shari's old mental and emotional programming.

"Reality" struck again one day as I sat at my desk paying bills. I subtracted a balance from the checkbook, and subtracted the next one, and the next. I soon realized that I had been only subtracting for the last several months, never depositing. No money was coming in and there was no guarantee that it ever would. I could see the end of our savings, the bottom of the barrel.

Shari's movie reel flickered on in my head again, fast forward, and the next thing I knew I was embroiled in insecurity. I just couldn't see how the financial situation would improve. As the feelings escalated, Donovan walked in my office and noticed, "You look a little frustrated."

I launched into a tirade. "I'm *more* than a little frustrated! What are we going to do for money? Nothing's coming in; everything's going out, and fast."

He tried to reassure me, "You know that we're always taken care of. We've never been without money. We'll know when the next opportunity comes along to earn a living." He pointed to the dwindling balance, "And look, we still have money from the sale of the house."

I interrupted him, "Yes! But what happens after *that's* gone?" My frustration accelerated into a vortex of panic. I ignored Donovan's reassurance. Finally, he just gave up and left the room while I sat alone, stewing. I *had* to do something about this situation. I had to do it now! The most logical solution, of course, was to get a job.

I went into my closet and rifled through everything, tossing one piece of clothing after another over my shoulder. Through a blur of tears I managed to find a nice navy blue dress and a pair of navy pumps, "Here's something that'll work!" I dug deep in a dresser drawer to find a pair of panty hose and assembled an outfit that looked professional and yet not too dressy. I was blindly driven to get a job in spite of the familiar faint voice that kept reassuring me, "Just walk through this. Soon you'll understand its purpose."

Donovan walked into the bedroom while I stepped into my heels, "Where are you going?"

Through my tears of despair I sputtered haltingly, "I'm going ... to get ... a job."

He tried to muffle a laugh. To him this was such an absurd reaction to a simple bill-paying task. "For years you've been the one telling me that we're always taken care of by the Universe, remember? We've always found a way to earn an income. Have you forgotten?"

I could vaguely remember what Donovan was talking about, yet at this moment handling the critical financial situation seemed more important. Maybe then I could relax and remember. By now the curtain had risen and I was well into the play. Here I was dressed up, made up, and mixed up all at once, determined to get a job that day.

I drove the 10 minutes into town. What kind of job could I get in a small town of about 12,000 people? We were so new to the area, I hardly knew where to begin. Then I remembered a small clothing boutique whose windows had caught my eye. I spoke to the owner and inquired whether she needed any help. "As a matter of fact, we *do* need some help. My best salesperson just quit. What do you know about the retail business?"

I fully clicked into my professional persona. To impress her with my vast experience I told her my work history. "I developed and implemented a wholesale floral supply business and managed a ski shop. I was also the principal of an entire school, and I know how to interact with people because I organized thousands of volunteers in the Special Olympics program."

She was delighted, "You're hired! When can you start?"

I absent-mindedly asked, "How much does the job pay anyway?"

"Given your experience, I can pay you over minimum wage, say $4.75 an hour."

By this time the euphoria of victory was wearing off and I began to sense that I looked ridiculous. "I need the evening to think about it and talk it over with my husband.

But I'll call you in the morning."

I got back in the car, drove one block and had to pull over. I was laughing so hysterically I couldn't control myself. I said out loud to myself, "You *are* employable, in case you needed to know that." This exercise was necessary for the human part of me and yet so *un*necessary for another part of me. I smiled to myself all the way home, tittering as I walked through the back door.

Donovan was waiting for me to tell him the news, "Well, how'd it go?"

"I got a job and can start tomorrow if I want it. ..." and explained the details.

"Well, are you going to take it?"

"No. I'm certain I'm not going to take it. I just had to play out the whole scenario for some strange reason. It's really not what I want. And I also remembered that I don't like wearing pumps!"

This whole process had unearthed core beliefs about money and security that lurked within Shari's subconscious. Her belief was that if she didn't get a job and earn a regular income she wouldn't have any money. She was convinced that if *she* didn't get a job, certainly nobody else in the household would. Without a regular, steady flow of income, she couldn't feel secure. Surely she would be reduced to begging on the street.

I realized I had to begin seriously to claim what was true for me, Juelle. I said to myself, "You *know* in a very deep part of your being that you are always supported by the Universe. You don't ever have to wonder or be afraid. Creating money is always part of the adventure of exploring what you love to do, what makes your heart sing. You'll always find a way for resources to flow through you. You get to discern, select from, and engage in possibilities that are in alignment with your inner knowing. You don't just sit around and wait for something to fall in your lap, nor do you have to 'muscle' or scramble around to find it. Somehow, some way, there will *always* be money there."

I would get many opportunities to practice the lesson I had just given to myself. I needed to remind myself of its great "Aha!" many times until it burned itself into all levels of my consciousness. After a while, Shari's inappropriate responses began to fade. Once old belief systems were changed at their core, I was free to modify old behavioral tendencies. I stopped reacting to meaningless external cues. A loud voice didn't scare the daylights out of me. My behavior was no longer dictated by anything outside of me.

I began to create a different kind of reality, a whole new vision based on following my Spirit. "I am surrounded by people who love me and support me just the way I am." I said to myself, "I know that my world is absolutely safe, and that I am always taken care of and guided by my own Spirit. I cannot make a mistake, so I can stop trying to get it right, out of fear that I might have it wrong. I am always doing the next thing, not the right thing or the wrong thing, but the next thing. And it is perfect just the way it is. I experience joy, abundance and fulfillment because I know that's where I came from."

As I sorted through all the subtle ways that Shari's past was operating in Juelle's present, Donovan was engaged in a deep spiritual realization of his own. He began to understand all that he was, including having a divine purpose. The tender spot in him opened up even more. At times he would be moved to tears by stories of the vastness of the human condition. He recognized the sacred dance of life as well as his own unique steps in it. Through an internal spiritual shift, he began to claim his part and to understand its value in the universe. The shift didn't show up so much in his behavior as it did in his attitudes, his self-confidence and his sense of peace.

He was finally able to lay his personal history to rest. He came to a place of peace about his parents' death, confident that he had done everything possible for them, for me, for Christian, for everyone in his life. Although he recognized that he was sometimes emotionally unavailable, and occasionally was not easy to live with during his protracted grief process, he finally accepted that he had done the best he could given his limited emotional resources at the time. He became much more compassionate toward others, as we all do when we come to accept more of ourselves. He understood the subtle dynamics of his own attitudes and behaviors that enabled him to allow others to be who they were, without judging their logic or the beliefs that filtered their reality.

As he quit placing difficult expectations on others, he experienced a greater allowance for himself. He developed a real and deep relationship with his own Spirit, his own divine aspect. He began to recognize what he was moved by his Spirit to do, and to follow that still small voice inside him without question, in spite of his personal preferences, and without attachment to a particular outcome.

For example, in his enthusiasm to guide Christian, he inadvertently imposed his well-meaning advice on her and naturally expected that she would follow it. After all, he had lived more of life; he knew what was true for him. He assumed, therefore, that it must also be true for her. Now he was able to pull back a little. He still offered her loving advice, but he was no longer attached to whether she heeded it.

This clearing process was essential for both of us. Our lives were no longer based upon a past reference point.

We began living in the present NOW, together, directed moment by moment into future possibilities. Cellular memory, dysfunctional behavior patterns and limiting belief systems no longer determined our lives. They were simply memories, catalysts to help us grow into our own Spirits of God presence. We both emerged from this period fully anchored in our own truth, and re-committed to our partnership and to our spiritual journey of service.

17

The
Channel

After four months, we began to assimilate our intense changes, and our lives smoothed out. Both Donovan and I settled in to our new home and I became more comfortable with the disparities in personal preferences between Shari and me. For instance, Shari loved to cook but I, on the other hand, wasn't much interested in it, so we needed to find a convenient way to prepare meals. We discovered the Schwan's truck that delivered freshly-prepared foods to our doorstep. It was a crisp spring morning when Dick, the delivery man, drove up in the familiar yellow refrigerator truck.

Donovan was away for a few days on a fishing trip to test the world's best lures that he bought in Nebraska. I decided to treat myself to my favorite ice cream, creamy praline, along with the usual order of vegetarian lasagna and cheese ravioli. As Dick yanked on the chrome handle and reached into a freezer compartment to pull out my box of ice cream, I noticed two little golden lab puppies, not more than two months old, scampering around the truck. "What cute puppies you have! What are their names?"

He looked up at me puzzled, "These aren't my puppies. I don't know where they came from."

"What? You mean you didn't bring them?"

"Nope. And I don't want to leave with them either. Good luck!"

I hated to think that someone had dumped the puppies out here, six miles from town. I went back inside and closed the door, sure that if I left them alone they'd find where they belonged farther up the road. As I moved through the house the puppies followed and watched me through the windows. I could see that they weren't going to leave me alone. I'd have to deal with them somehow. Donovan would be gone for another three days, which gave me some time to figure out what to do. If he got home and saw these adorable puppies, we'd surely have to keep them even though we didn't want the responsibility, additional cost and work of raising and training two puppies.

I accepted my mission. I went out in the backyard to bring them a pan of water. Wherever they had been before they were obviously well cared for. They appeared to be plump and well-fed with shiny, golden coats. They bounded over to me and licked me, friendly and unafraid. As they romped with each other, I sat on the lawn in the morning sunlight and weighed my options. "I can try to find them homes, but I don't know that many people here. I could put an ad in the paper, but it doesn't come out for another few days and who knows how long it will take from there? I could take them to the dog pound. They're so cute, I'm sure someone would want them. No! I can't do that! That's definitely not an option."

I called upon the skills that Shari employed at the

Pura Vida kennel in Costa Rica. I made the puppies a place
to sleep in the roomy shed where the previous owners had
kept their dog. It was totally fenced in, dry and warm. I scat-
tered a bed of straw in a large cardboard box and gave them
my old horse blanket to sleep on. The kennel kept them safe
from cars on the road and coyotes in the nearby woods. I put
their water bowl inside and went to town to buy a bag of
puppy food.

On the way to town the decision became clear. I
would do what I could to find them each a new home. When
I returned with a 20-pound bag of kibble, I let the puppies
out of the shed so that I could get a sense of their personalities. I wanted them to have a home that suited their
temperaments and the best way to get to know them was to
observe and interact with them. They were so carefree in
their expression of life. Everything was fascinating to them.
With innocent awe and wonder they discovered insects,
sticks and a rubber ball.

I suddenly realized that I had just spent four intense
months working through the cellular memory of Shari's life
history. These puppies were my gift from Spirit to remind
me that we have all come from joy. We are joy. The puppies
brought back childlike appreciation to my world. They
brought back fun. My heart sang! A part of me was reborn
into the joy of emergence. They helped me remember that I
was intended to live every day of my life this way. I thanked
God for sending me these two little golden beings and for
giving me this assignment.

The next day, Saturday, I had an appointment to get
my hair cut. I told the stylist about how the two beautiful
little golden lab pups found their way to my doorstep. A
woman at the counter paying her bill obviously overheard
me telling the story. She walked over to me. "My daughter

has three young children, who've been wanting to get a golden lab. Would you mind if I call her and tell her about your puppies?"

"Mind? Of course not! I'll even go home to get the puppies and take them to your daughter's house so that she can see them."

I went home, loaded up the puppies, their bag of food and their blanket, constructed a sign that read "Free puppy to a good home" and headed back into town. I drove to the lady's daughter's house and carried one puppy under each arm to her fenced-in back yard. She let loose her three children under the age of eight and I let loose my two puppies under the age of eight weeks and we watched the fun. I interviewed the mother to make sure that whichever one they chose would get a good home and kind treatment. The little female cuddled up to the children. This was obviously her new home. The children jumped up and down, squealing with delight, "What shall we name her, Mommy?" I was so happy for that little puppy! I kissed her good-bye and thanked her for the wonderful gift she had given me.

I picked up the little male puppy, put him next to me in the front seat and drove to the supermarket. I found a strategic place to sit outside the doors, gathered the puppy up in my arms, and propped the sign against the wall. Exhausted from cavorting with the children, he rested his head on my shoulder and snoozed between visitors. For the next hour and a half, no one came out or went in to the store who didn't admire the puppy. They cooed over him. "Oh, I wish I could take him!" "That's a little golden lab! He's so cute." The puppy blinked open his eyes to acknowledge his fans and then fell back asleep.

Just then a lady came by who looked to be in her

sixties, probably retired. She stroked the puppy's head tenderly and asked me questions about him. She offered every excuse under the sun about why she couldn't take him, the same excuses I had heard all morning. Then she asked me a question that no one else had asked. "Do you mind if I hold him?"

"Of course not. Here." I handed her the sleepy puppy. He snuggled up to her then suddenly opened his eyes wide and began licking her face.

She nuzzled him and spoke softly to him. I could feel her will power dissolve. Then she quickly shoved the puppy back at me and said, "I just can't take a dog now," and scurried away.

I thought to myself, "This puppy belongs to that woman. Why doesn't she see that? He perked up more with her than with anyone else this whole day. How can she walk away from him? He's obviously hers."

We stood outside the grocery store for another hour and a half, a pair of eager greeters. I couldn't believe my eyes! The same woman came out of the door again. She walked over to me and studied the puppy intently. I stood there silently, trying not to interrupt her train of thought.

Suddenly she exclaimed, "I just can't have a puppy right now!" as though she were trying to convince herself, and quickly walked away.

Surprisingly, I found myself following her to her car. As she loaded her groceries into the trunk I asked, "Why can't you have this puppy right now? It sure looks like you want him and I know that he wants you. He responded to you much more than anyone else we've seen all day."

She turned to me with tears in her eyes. "I don't have enough money to give this dog the kind of care that I would want to give him. And I'm dying of cancer. I don't have very long to be here. I just can't have a dog."

I looked deeply into her sad eyes, and with a lump in my throat I managed to say, "That's exactly the reason why you need this dog. He wants to be with you now ... ."

Tears streamed down her cheeks. She lifted the puppy out of my arms, and held him close to her, "Well ... we'll just give it a try then, won't we little guy?"

I was overwhelmed with compassion. "Just a minute! Let me run back to the car, I have his bag of dog food and blanket." I went back to my car and quickly scooped up his belongings, along with a twenty dollar bill.

I put the puppy supplies in the passenger seat of her car and pressed the money into her hand. "Here, this is for getting the puppy his shots."

"Oh, no, you don't really need to do this."

"No, it's not a need. I want to. This puppy was a gift to me, too." I watched her fluff up the blanket and make the puppy comfortable on the seat next to her. I wanted to race away before she could see my tears. Before I could move, she put her arms around me and sighed, "I can't thank you enough. You can be sure that he'll have a wonderful home."

I cried tears of joy all the way home. I was filled with gratitude for the precious moments of life that remind us who we really are. This was as profound a mystical experience as any I had ever encountered in my life. Two little puppies had delivered the gifts. They reminded me that all of life is a joyful experience, and that divine messengers come in many forms.

The puppies also prompted me to remember that Donovan and I had been such messengers in our clients' lives in Montana. It was as natural for us as it was for the puppies. We were designed to do it. As an articulator, I could not *not* do it. Offering spiritual counseling sessions was one of the ways we could contribute the most. We loved to help people to live the lives they were born to live, to remember who they are, to embody a state of divinity. Donovan and I happened to be the messengers, and it was as great a gift to us as it was to our clients. We made a conscious declaration, "We are hereby available and ready to go back to work."

The very next day we received a phone call from a woman whom he had met at a workshop he attended the previous year. "It was hard to track you two down," she said. "But I'm ready to have an intensive session with you. I hope you're still providing the service." That's all it took, we were back at work. This session led to a workshop and then another. More people began calling us for private sessions. Within two months I began depositing money into the checking account again.

Our circle of acquaintances widened to include Veronica and Joseph, a fun-loving couple whose lives were dedicated to spiritual pursuits. Veronica was a sought-after psychic, and Joseph was a hands-on energy healer. Theirs was a light-hearted spirituality. Time with them always had a sense of devotion punctuated by human whimsy. Conversations were never boring. We jumped from talking about the ancient mystery schools, to life in New York, to organizing the largest psychic fair in the United States, to eliminating fat from our diets. These two were always at the hub of social activities.

Kathleen called us and invited us to Veronica and Joseph's gathering on the next Sunday afternoon. "I'm giving a channeling session and I'd like you two to come."

"Yes, of course, we'd love to be there."

We drove to Veronica and Joseph's spiritual retreat center at the base of Mount Rainier, through budding trees and horse fields dotted with crocus and daffodils. Veronica offered a prayer to receive the highest spiritual blessing, and Joseph offered a meditation to relax us into an altered state of divine consciousness. With every word, the hum of daily life faded away as I sank into a deep peacefulness. Then, I noticed a strange sensation. My head filled up with a force that put pressure on the third eye and at the base of my head, and the same heat I felt in my hands during healing sessions. It surged through my entire body. I began to jerk, lurch and rock involuntarily, almost as though my frequency were being adjusted to handle an energy expansion.

Somewhere off in the distance I could hear Kathleen say, "Juelle looks like she's going to channel." It was a most peculiar moment, almost like an overlay reality. I knew that my eyes were closed and yet I could look around the room and see it, and everyone in it, with razor-sharp clarity.

This energy wasn't foreign to me at all. I had felt it before, often. Its essence embodied peace and the grandeur of cosmic divine order. Nothing inside my personality was afraid, only reluctant. This time, the fullness of the force desired to be expressed. I could hear it clairaudiently and I could see the words that it wanted to speak. Soon my mouth was full of them. I was instructed to open it and let them come out. My personality resisted, "No, I don't want to open my mouth, I don't want to let these words out."

I felt as if I were in a dream, at the same time aware that it was a dream, and yet compelled to dream it anyway. I sensed Joseph coming closer to me, quietly reassuring me, "It's okay, Juelle. There's an entity who wants to channel through you. Just open your mouth and let it come through."

With his assurance, my ego, the "I" part of me, willingly stepped aside. I opened my mouth and heard a strange voice say, "Yes. Hello. We are here now."

The people in the room greeted the voice coming out of me one after another. "Hello." "Welcome."

I sensed the energy look through my closed eyes and deeply into the people gathered to welcome it. My personality was having its own reaction, bewildered, curious and yet strangely calm.

I heard Joseph say, "Well, who *are* you?"

The voice responded, "Yes. We are the Master Saint Germain."

I immediately recognized the voice. It had been with me all these years. I had heard it inside my ears, inside my heart, and inside my being. This was the energy that had assisted me through my transformation, and before that, Shari's memory confirmed that it had bolstered her in her spiritual discoveries.

I inquired internally, "Why have you chosen to speak in this form, through me?"

Saint Germain answered, "Because it's just time in your personal evolution to do so. This is one of many ways that you can be utilized by Spirit, in service."

I was so engrossed in my own internal dialogue with St. Germain that I barely remember him answering questions posed by people in the room.

In any event, he only remained for a short time, then departed. "We are complete for now." My consciousness returned. The sense of fullness in my body abated along with the pressure inside my head. I opened my eyes in total disbelief about what had happened. I came to this event to support Kathleen, never once considering that *I* might actually channel an entity *myself.* I felt shy, embarrassed and self-conscious.

Because the experience was such a graceful and comfortable entry for this energy, I questioned its authenticity. Communicating such a familiar benevolent being didn't seem dramatic or unusual, so I thought that it must have been my own fabrication. "Was that *real?* Was it really *true?*" Yet I was convinced that it was. I recognized the energy so intimately.

Kathleen said, "When you are attuned, available and resonating with the entities who wish to work through you it is a very loving and expansive experience. It certainly isn't strange or difficult at all."

Although I knew that what she said was true, I still found myself in a whirl. Later, I came to discover that walk-ins often come in with talents and gifts not present in the former inhabitant such as psychic abilities, creative and healing abilities, as well as channeling abilities. These are natural to the new Spirit, along with different goals and ambitions, personality traits and personal preferences.

This event set in motion a series of *conscious* interactions with Saint Germain. I sensed that channeling would be a natural part of my life because the familiar voice of an entire life span, both Shari's and mine, was finally able to speak through me to others.

18

A New
Reality

Over the next few months, Donovan and I invited friends and acquaintances to gather at our home to evoke messages from and interact with the channeled entity. During these initial sessions, I was intensely reluctant to let the entity through my mental, emotional and physical structures. "What will people think? What will they say? What if the entity says something that people don't like? What if it says something that I don't like?"

But channeling in a comfortable environment enabled me to allow these frequencies through with greater ease. Sensing my reluctance, someone in the initial group very kindly said, "Juelle, tell your physical body that it won't be killed if you allow these energies to speak through you." Grateful for the suggestion, I told my physical body, "It's okay. You don't have to worry about being harmed in any way if Spirit chooses to be expressed in this form." I realized that I had cellular memories stored in my consciousness of gruesome deaths in past lives, of having been burned at the stake as a witch and having been imprisoned for speaking my truth. I understood that the woman in the Akashic slide show walking to the guillotine was condemned for appearing to be demon-possessed. These past-life memories had been locked in this body, encoding fear into its very cells. Their influence affected my body's sense of safety and longevity and caused my reluctance to put myself in jeopardy, to be rejected, tortured or even murdered.

Saint Germain vibrated a unique pattern. I also noticed many other distinctively different vibrational frequencies belonging to other entities. Saint Germain identified his personal resonance during my first channeling session. He never mentioned his name again. Nor did any of the others. I asked them how they wished to be identified. "We prefer to be identified as 'The Council of Twelve.' We do not wish to be identified as particular entities because people become attached to a name or to a personality and miss the message that is carried here." The Council explained their purpose for channeling through me. "We are here to illuminate the pathways home, to illuminate the God consciousness in all things. We are here to assist all people in awakening to their true spiritual destinies as divine human beings, merging Heaven and Earth."

As I sat in deep contemplation, a slow realization crept in around the edges of my thoughts that grew into a magnificent "Aha!" It was The Council who had assisted me through those first few days of despair. "You were the ones who explained to Sylvia what had happened during the actual walk-in experience! You were the energy that buoyed me up when I felt like I was drowning in confusion! Isn't that so?"

"Yes, indeed. And simultaneously we were making

energetic adjustments in your new body, assisting it to accommodate the increased frequencies that Juelle energy brought into it."

I came to understand that The Council was available to me at any moment. All I had to do was close my eyes and focus my entire attention and energy to a single point in consciousness. During a channeling session, my personality says "Yes," the group in the room says "Yes," and the entities composing The Council say "Yes." The spiritual spigot turns on and the energy begins to flow. It is that natural and automatic.

After a particularly lively and interactive session, I was curious about any physical changes that may have taken place when I channeled so I asked Donovan, "What do I look like when I'm channeling?"

He thought about it momentarily and answered, "It's hard to describe. Overall, you look the same but you speak with a different accent which I can't identify. When you speak you use words and concepts that you don't normally use in everyday language. And you talk louder, by far. Your eyes either clamp shut or squint open in narrow slits and your face seems to broaden into a wide smile. You sit forward in the chair, sometimes leaning into the group, using wide gestures. What does all this feel like on the inside?"

I thought about my answer, and said, "That's a difficult question. It's sort of like asking, 'How does it feel to breathe?' My whole personality steps aside and I'm filled with an all-loving energy. I become expanded awareness and lose a sense of separateness and a sense of my body. So I'm unaware of how my face changes or how my body moves. It seems that I have expanded vision, I can perceive a vastness even though I may peer through slits. I have my own interaction with the entities. I can hear their voices through me as a single voice talking to the group while I'm talking to them at the same time. I have a deeper under- standing of the words they use because I can hear them, see them and sense them all at once. When I first heard The Council, my personality was full of questions: 'Why are you talking about this? What's important here?' But somehow, the entities always weave a tight tapestry of concepts and words. So I've given up questioning what gets discussed and how."

Donovan nodded his head and asked, "After a session when you come back to full consciousness do you remember what was discussed?"

"Not really," I said. "At the time it's happening I'm totally aware of everything, but when I come back into my conscious awareness I'm left with only a sense of it, like awakening from a dream. For a few fleeting moments I can remember some details, but they soon become sketchy. And I always feel energized and magnificent afterward."

I was curious about why the particular entities that composed The Council were channeling through me. They helped my understand that different people who provide a channel attract different entities based on their natural inter- ests and experiences. For instance, a person who likes to talk about the physical universe will attract entities who have both the scientific language and background to facili- tate the flow of this particular kind of information into the world. The entities who are attracted to me were in align- ment with what's available in my collective experience and understanding to deliver.

For example, I care deeply about the evolution of the planet, about manifesting divinity through each and every person on it, so I attract those entities who are interested in assisting in that transformation.

I have no interest in attracting, allowing or channeling anything other than the highest possibility as directed by my Spirit of God. A disembodied Spirit living in another dimension and not in a human body may have a broader view of things, but it's not necessarily wiser or more altruistic. "As above, so below" means that it's still necessary to discern among energies as we would people whom we would invite into our lives. I'm simply not available to channel distorted or fear-based energies, only clear, benevolent messengers of Spirit.

Channeling became an organic part of our lives, naturally expanding into the spiritual counseling sessions we were already offering to clients. Through this process, I understood that Shari had been channeling in her own way for years. So long ago, when her personality stepped aside and she spoke so passionately and eloquently about the Special Olympics, I now recognized it as her distinctive form of channeling. Only the form in which I channel now has changed, not the essence of it.

Everyone "channels" in one way or another. Artists, writers, composers, engineers, teachers, inventors, healers, psychics all channel through their work. Sometimes people say that they are channeling their Spirit or "higher self." For instance, almost everyone as been available to say just the right comforting or inspirational words to a friend, without knowing where they came from. In order to solve a problem or find an answer, we often go to bed at night and dream about the solution or awaken with an inspiration. Scientists and researchers in different parts of the world will often invent something, or find a cure for a disease at virtually the same time.

During the course of our evolution, information has become available to the mass consciousness and has dropped in in the form of inspirations or ideas which have been picked up and uniquely channeled into the world. For example, popular culture reflects potential human transformation in works such as *Star Trek*. One episode of the TV series was called "The Transfiguration" in which a human-appearing being literally transformed into a body of light. *Close Encounters of the Third Kind* reminded us that we may not be alone in our evolutionary leaps and that we are surrounded by other life forms in the universe. *Cocoon* portrayed a group of light beings who effortlessly donned garments of human form to engage with life on planet Earth. *ET* personified our intense yearning for "home" and the recognition that we are all returning to the heart of God, our true cosmic origin. *Field of Dreams* showed us how to hold onto our vision no matter what.

If we build a new world for ourselves because something inside us moves us so strongly to do so, then "they will come." In other words, others will be inspired to build their visions of a new world as well. These, as well as avant-garde programming such as *The X-Files,* are just a few of the many examples of popular entertainment forms dealing with humanity's spiritual evolution and relationship with the mysteries of the universe.

I believe, everyone has a "council," so to speak. Some people refer to them as "guardian angels" or "Spirit guides," but every one of us has beings who are assigned to assist and to support us along our soul's journey. "The Council" just happened to be the group assigned to me. This form of channeling is one of the ways they interact with me and with others. It seemed very natural to me. The Council never imposed itself against my will; they never impinged on my personal sovereignty in any way. And yet they were always available to me.

I called on my Council to help me resolve a pressing issue concerning my integration into Shari's body, "I still notice some clumsiness," I said, "when I speak in terms of 'I.' Is it 'I' according to Shari's memory? Or is it 'I' according to Juelle now? Although Shari's memories are a part of the wholeness that I am, they don't always feel like me. When I speak to people and make reference to 'my childhood,' for instance, I can't claim it as mine at all. Even though all of those experiences are available for total recall, they don't feel accurate in the truth of who I am *now*."

I was led to understand that relatively speaking, six months of intensive adjustment in a new body was a short period of time to work through deep cellular memory and to stabilize a new identity. I was reminded that ordinarily it takes years, even lifetimes, to move through dysfunctional patterns. "You have chosen an accelerated training program."

Though humanity has lived through 'original pain' individually for centuries so that the planet can experience its deepest densities, that form of evolution is too slow during a period when time is accelerating. It is possible for me and for everyone else to trade in painful lessons for instantaneous realizations.

I began to understand with a deeper comprehension that Shari left me with fertile spiritual ground along with earthly practicality. That combination enabled me to relate to the world and to others on a very human level. Reference to 'the previous inhabitant's memory' or 'Shari's life,' was *absolutely* necessary for me to be able to solidly take a stand in who I was *now*. The Council suggested that it would become more graceful over time and with practice.

So over the next year I practiced. I practiced asserting my own spiritual identity. The more I practiced the more I began to remember who I was before I donned Shari's body, and why I came here. I felt the need to be spiritually fierce about taking a stand in Juelle. It seemed crucial to my identity to distinguish myself from Shari. I consciously practiced interacting with people in my own manner, even if I risked losing their friendship.

For instance, my old college friend Patsy came to visit. Shari's way to entertain guests had been to collect brochures, map out a detailed itinerary of highlights to visit to fill up the guest's week, and drive around to each one while describing all the salient details. She did this even if she didn't feel like it. Instead, I fanned out the brochures on the kitchen table and said, "Here are the brochures describing all the things you can do in Washington. Donovan and I aren't interested in going to see them again but we'll be here when you get back." Patsy looked shocked and surprised. She decided not to go either. She chose to share a week's worth of life with us, including attending a Council channeling session.

Because Donovan and I had moved to a new location and our lives changed, naturally, some people with whom we'd previously shared our lives fell away. But some old friends would still call or come for visits. Each time I re-evaluated whether this was a relationship I wanted to carry over to my present life. In most cases it was. Sometimes I would be moved to tell them the story and reveal that I was a walk-in. At other times I was not moved to do so. Sometimes they were puzzled. Sometimes they were fascinated. Sometimes they felt deserted or abandoned. Sometimes they weren't sure if they liked Juelle. Sometimes they didn't judge at all.

I could see that it was often uncomfortable and confusing for them when I talked about "Shari's" experiences. Nevertheless, I had to speak my truth about it. I asked them to call me "Juelle." In every case they did their best to honor my request. Because they naturally expected me to respond to them in the way that Shari did, they were sometimes surprised when I didn't.

As I adopted my own way of being and didn't treat the walk-in experience as other than normal, I noticed that everyone else followed suit. I chuckled to myself, remembering how Donovan had so aptly described me. "Shari was like a Corvette, sleek, shiny, finely-tuned, beautiful and fast," he said. "You are all of the above with one major difference; four-wheel drive. You are unstoppable. You can go anywhere!"

Over time, just as The Council predicted, adjusting to physical life became easier. After two years of being here as Juelle, something just suddenly clicked and I completely relaxed into what I call "my life," which honored Shari's life experiences and her responses to them, as well as my own life experiences and my responses to them. From that point forward I could use the pronoun "I" to encompass both. As I began to speak more freely about being a walk-in, people invariably asked me, "Where did Shari go? Was it just too difficult for her to continue here? Did she give up?"

I *knew* that she didn't give up, but I needed more specific information. I took the question to The Council for some insights. They explained in simple terms what took place: "The Spirit of Shari left her body for another assignment, or expression, on a different dimension. The Spirit that you are, identified as 'Juelle,' did indeed walk-in. You are a completely different entity. And we wish to repeat once again: The agreement between two spirits, one to walk in and one to walk out, is *always* a clear agreement, made at

the soul level, within the divine plan. In your case, Shari
was conscious at some level that she was leaving because
she clearly completed her portion of the mission. She did
not leave mid-stream."

The explanation the Council made convinced me
that Shari had tidied up her life before she left. She had
graciously made preparation for my entry. Her valuable
legacy was a rich storehouse of memories and a detailed
reference library of living life on planet Earth as she knew
it. It was given to me to take advantage of Shari's advanced
learning and adaptation to life, and to function here quite
easily because of her experiences and her keen sense of
observation and discernment.

I understood finally that she left, comfortable in the
knowing that at some level I, the walk-in, would be as
graceful and compatible as possible with the major relationships she had prepared: with a husband, Donovan, a
man with deep mystical understanding of life, and with a
daughter, Christian, a woman who held earthly traditions
for me to share. My Spirit, which came in as Juelle, was
fully equipped and resonated sympathetically with all major
aspects of Shari's life. Spirit, I realized with a profound
sense of humility, never wastes anything.

I was overcome with wonder. I was on Earth with a
predisposition to accelerate the mission Shari had started. I
brought with me a remembrance of my interdimensional
awareness and an undaunting force for the co-creation of
heaven on Earth. The Council's words rang through my
being with profound understanding. The message I received
was potent; it was imprinted as indelible truth in the fiber of
my being. The Council confirmed my assignment as a
"householder," a bridge between heaven and Earth.

About a year later, in late October, we received a

telephone call from Aunt Anna. She told us that my father had died. He shot himself in the heart with a deer hunting rifle. By this time, my father had long-divorced Beverly and was in the advanced stages of alcoholism, living in a drunken state during most of his waking hours, and suffering from intense delirium tremens every morning until he threw back a few shots of whiskey. He was experiencing severe depression due to his physical deterioration and intense pain. I was struck by the irony that he could rig up a rifle to successfully shoot himself in the heart, the place where he probably hurt the most.

We drove to Michigan for the funeral to be held three days later on Halloween, All Souls' Day. I was in and out of a dazed shock, laced with grief. I always knew that he wouldn't live long, probably dying of complications of alcoholism, but I never dreamed that he would take his own life.

During the long drive, my mind took a sentimental journey, meandering through the memories of this man I had willingly assimilated as a part of my wholeness. I realized that I was on my way to the center of a former life. All the relatives and acquaintances would be gathered, calling me "Shari" and projecting her identity upon me. We arrived in time to go to the funeral home. The minute I walked in, Aunt Anna sprang to her feet, "Shari's here!" I was instantly swarmed by aunts, uncles, cousins and friends. After embracing each one and remembering his or her place in the family tree, I stepped aside to view my father, laid out in his full American Legion uniform. His fellow Legionnaires would escort him to his final resting place with taps and the usual gun salute.

I was relieved for this man. I knew how much he loved me even though it was always unspoken. No matter how many times I forgave him, I knew that he never forgave himself for not coming to my rescue from my brutal mother. Nor did he forgive himself for not living up to his own expectations of what a good Amish son should be, and for not being able to control his addiction. I honored the choices that he had made. Even though I didn't understand them, I knew that they were somehow perfect for who he was and for his soul's journey. Maybe his last desperate act was the only way he knew of saying, "I've had enough. No more pain." At last it was over. He was at peace.

An uncle came up alongside me and looked down at his brother's body, shaking his head, "What a shame. What a shame. It was a rough time for him."

I looked up at him and clarified, "Yes, it was a rough time for him. But it wasn't a shame. He did the best he could. And right up to the very end, he did the best he knew how to do. But his life wasn't a shame."

The day after the funeral, before Donovan and I returned home, all the relatives gathered at Cousin David's house for a pot-luck dinner in our honor. Everyone was there, Aunt Anna, Uncle Eli, Cousin Marie, her husband and their three children, David, his wife and child, Beverly, even Ronnie and his family. Everyone. I never told any of them that I was a walk-in. It wasn't necessary, I didn't have to prove who I was. I knew who I was. I'd already taken a firm stand in it. I was free simply to honor the truth and to let it be.

Before I left for this trip, I had wondered how I would feel about these people. I wondered if I would love them as much as Shari did. My eyes roamed from one person to the next, to the next. Such intense love and honor welled up inside of me for every single one. As I gazed around that table, I knew that the number of times our paths would physically cross again would be very few, if at all.

But it didn't change how much I loved them and appreciated the valuable part they played in my early life. With deep gratitude, I silently thanked and blessed each one.

And I was so grateful to have my nuclear family. Christian was grown and living a happy and independent life. Donovan and I experienced mature love and commitment based on mutual respect that was more than a personal relationship. It was a nurturing partnership founded upon a strong knowing that we were here in service to the planet together. Shari had worked psychologically, emotionally and spiritually to clear the negativity of fear and pain in her life. She had claimed her own essence and defined what she wanted in life, rather than allowing her experiences to dictate the limits of what she could have and what she could be.

She gave me a great gift. She never waited for life to embrace her; she embraced life. She raced for it. By consistently putting herself forward she lived a full experience of God presence upon the Earth. So often, if we don't have a guru, if we haven't had a mystical experience, if we're not a walk-in, we somehow feel spiritually limited. We therefore can only go so far. By waiting for a golden being to touch us and bestow upon us immediate enlightenment, we miss the opportunity to engage with life, to participate in it to the nth degree. Shari's zest for life was a magnificent jewel tucked inside this package that was me. I use it daily. It returns sparkling surprises and value beyond measure.

I felt such deep appreciation for the part she had played here. Her life, with its myriad experiences equipped me with vast resources from which to draw. Indeed, she served beautifully. Shari was a dedicated spiritual adventurer compelled by her own love of God presence. By exploring many paths, she forged one of clear light that enabled me to enter a purified sanctuary through which I now could devote a lifetime of holy service.

On the journey home, I realized that every single person at the dinner table the previous night was part of me. All of Shari's memories were a part of me. The landscape parading by the car window, the mountains, the farm houses, the cities and the unique life experiences inside them were also a part of me. Whatever happened in someone's back yard on the other side of the globe somehow affected what happened in my back yard.

Earth life can distort reality and contribute to a sense of separateness by establishing territories, boundaries between this person and that one, between this country and that one, even between this planet and that one. My mission was to embrace all of it, knowing that I came from infinite oneness, and that I would return to infinite oneness; that is all.

19

My
Purpose

I come from a golden world where love, peace and joy are not emotional experiences, but rather a state of being, an "IS-ness." It is a world, not of matter, but limitless. golden light. We move from place to place in our own crafted-in-consciousness light vehicles. We recognize one another by the unique radiance of the living light that we are. And so are you.

Since we are nomadic in nature, my world is not a planet or a place. We move our entire world from dimension to dimension, from planet to planet, dissolving and re-creating to fit the requirements of the dimension we are assigned to. And so do you.

To enter this planet, I have dropped through many dimensional portals and "walked in" through a "doorway" to the Earth plane. Though I am aware of my origins, I am like all of us here. I am human. I am subject to the pull of third-dimensional density and the distortions of mass consciousness. I have emotional ups and downs, ins and outs. I have likes and dislikes. I do silly things. I get mad, have fun, and every now and then I think that something is really important and that it matters. I'm still learning and growing. Yet always, I know who I am. And I know my own truth. I know that there is more to me than the day-to-day human drama. And so it is with you.

I honor the sovereignty of all living things. Therefore, I come here not to take a stand *against* anything or anyone. Rather, I come to take a stand *for* something. I *stand for the facilitation of future reality, and so do you.*

These are the end times. As a world, we are moving to a consciousness where hate, fear, limitation and separateness will not exist. That future may be difficult to imagine when everything appears to be worse on the planet than ever before: violence, distortions, greed, sexual preoccupation, failed relationships and the dissolution of economic, governmental, educational and social structures. That which is unwieldy and out of alignment always has to be transformed. Sometimes it has to shift and collapse to allow a greater reality. We are now feeling the contractions of the birth canal, hailing the end of the Piscean Age and the emergence of the phoenix rising, the Aquarian Age, where new models of coexistence, co-creation and service will be born.

The planetary situation perfectly reflects the microcosm of our personal lives. Only when they appear to be falling apart are we catalyzed into action, to stand up and say, "ENOUGH!" Enough violence, enough abuse, enough poverty, enough sensationalism, enough hate. Both on the personal and global levels we are simply moving past the boundaries we identified as ourselves and expanding into something more.

Now is the time for all of us to claim our divine, rightful places in the universe. In order to do so, we must love ourselves enough to allow it to happen. And we must love one another enough to care about what happens in our neighborhoods, both literally and metaphorically. The time has come again to quicken the notion of *namasté,* "the God in me honors the God in you." If every single person recognized himself or herself as a living light of God embodied in human form and began to honor that aspect of themselves, then began to see that same aspect of God in all others, *the world would transform in an instant.*

The cosmic time clock is going off now. We are on the brink of an evolutionary leap in consciousness, a dimensional shift from an old world based on fear and limitation to a new world based upon infinite love, infinite beauty, joy, peace, abundance and oneness. Now is the time for us to awaken, on a massive scale, from our slumber of forgetfulness and to lift the veil of the illusion of separateness to reveal our true spiritual identity, our own divinity.

As we approach the evolutionary leap, information pre-encoded in our cellular memory is being activated, and we are remembering. We all carry a divine blueprint that maps our pathway to ascended consciousness. The flower of ascension will open into full bloom near the end of the millennium. And we come together at this time to assist one another in awakening and to *remember* messages which have been encoded in the very fiber of our souls. These messages are of:

• **Oneness:** We are moving from a fear-based, survival reality of separation to a love-based reality that expresses our true, divine, essential nature of infinite oneness. In this reality we will recognize that we are a part of a whole. We will see our individual consciousness merging into the Universal mind as separation dissolves and unification evolves. We are never alone. We are always attended by our Spirit, our councils, our angels, and inter-

dimensional entities and energies which assist us, along
with friends, family, and those we don't even know. The
process includes the clerk at the grocery store or the local
artist who can contribute to who we are simply by being
who they are.

• **Purpose:** It is not an accident that we are all here
at this time. Somewhere in our soul's divine plan we made
an awesome choice among all the dimensions, planets and
universes to be HERE, NOW. We have selected our unique
part to play in this grand drama, to be an integral part of a
whole that is larger than ourselves. We assist in planetary
transformation not by discovering a cure for cancer or
AIDS, or by solving world hunger, but by concentrating on
our own lives and sharing it with those in our address book,
office or community. So often we do nothing because the
task seems so daunting and we feel so small in the face of
it. But as we heal, forgive and transform aspects of our own
lives, we automatically offer healing and transformation to
a larger reality. As we each awaken into Divine Love, all
awaken. Therefore, we each make a profound difference.

• **Love and allowance:** We are reminded simply to
love one another with a love that transcends personal love,
a love that is larger than oneself. It is a kind, non-judgmental, allowing, unconditional love, with no attachment to
the outcome. It is also a love of self as a spark of Divinity.
For we are all alive here and now to embody the frequency
of Divine Love, and to anchor it on Earth as we move into
Unity Consciousness. Allowance is the first step to unconditional love. It's logical that all people will always act
according to their beliefs and the emotional/psychological
resources available to them. To serve them, and remarkably
to serve ourselves at the same time, we must not judge them
as good/bad, right/wrong, better than/less than, or expect

them to give or to understand something they simply cannot. We must allow others to be who they are without attempting to change them. They are who they are. But most of all, we must stop judging *ourselves. This is the true expression of love.*

• **Discernment:** When we judge one another's uniqueness, story, path and purpose, we are in separation. Instead, all of us must develop the capacity to discern what is beneficial and true for *ourselves*. What is useful to us serves our higher purpose. What is not useful to us does not serve us, and therefore we are not fully available to serve those around us. Discern in every single moment, "What is mine to do?" "Is this beneficial for me?" "Does this evoke more of who I am?" We may not be in alignment with a particular path or story and therefore choose not to have it in our lives. But we can allow that, somehow, somewhere, it may serve someone else perfectly. Discernment is, therefore, a form of love of self and honor for all that is.

• **Joy:** We come from joy and we return home to joy. Why not experience joy in the meantime? We can grant ourselves some ease and playfulness as we fulfill our divine destinies. It really isn't as serious as we make it. Consider how light our life would be if we treated it like a hobby. A hobby is what we passionately love, what we do in our free time, what flows easily, what creates more energy than it uses. Imagine what might happen if we shifted our focus from separating work and play and allow it all to become play! Imagine if we remembered the awe and wonder of childhood discoveries. As expressions of God, our evolution was meant to be a case-study in joy.

• **Gifts:** We are all yearning to express our "true" work. It is simply this: whatever brings us joy and makes our heart sing. If we remain open to the gifts and talents of

Spirit flowing through us and keep engaging in them, we will eventually be led to an expression of "work" that is most suitable for us and our unique design. Even though there are billions of people with unique talents and skills to invent new technologies, new ways of relating and new ideas, our own gifts are awakening within us at this moment. We must trust that they have value in the world and they will be utilized to empower others, to help them awaken and remember.

• **Abundance and support:** Ignite in one another the profound knowing that we are truly supported, by living our lives according to divine direction, aware that we are always guided to fulfill our unique destiny. It defies law to think that we won't be supported in every way to fulfill that destiny. Therefore we must remember that we are always at the perfect place, at the perfect time, doing the perfect thing, with the perfect people, and have all the resources, EVERY-THING, that we need in order to do it.

The natural world has an inner knowing that it functions flawlessly. A plant does not need to believe in photosynthesis to turn green. It is green. A fish doesn't need to know about oxygen to breathe. Its very configuration automatically gleans oxygen from its environment. Similarly, we have not come here to build a new world with only a hammer and one nail. We have a diverse team using old and new technologies to implement fresh ideas. We must keep our eyes open and recognize what Spirit brings into our lives so that we can co-create even more resources to circulate back through the system. When the "chi" energy in our bodies does not move, it lodges in the muscles and bones and creates pain. Similarly, if the planet's abundance is hoarded and not circulated, someone, somewhere will feel the pain of being cut off from its resources. Greed and lack are caused by an underlying fear that we are not supported by the Universe. We absolutely *must* come to trust our divine, rightful place at the table of abundance in order to be free to share it with others.

• **Peace and freedom:** All we ever want is a deep peacefulness in our lives and freedom from all that appears to be keeping us from it. We imply lack when we say, "If only I had my right livelihood, my life's purpose, my perfect soul mate, vibrant health, more money, a BMW, the perfect body," etc. What is perfect about our lives NOW? Someone said, "Peace is not the absence of conflict, but the presence of God." There is freedom in forgiving our past, releasing our enemies, letting down our walls and letting go of blame and guilt. There is peace in embracing grace, the influence of the Spirit of God operating in all of us. For grace can regenerate and strengthen us, quiet our minds and make whole once again our broken hearts.

• **Hopes and Dreams:** We are on the brink of a shining new humanity, a magnificent, grand spiritual awakening taking place *right now.* All who are awakening carry the message of hope. As we push through self-imposed boundaries and limitations, others can experience expansion as well. As we shine a light of compassion, free of judgment, upon our own lives, our planet and our world, others will be uplifted in hope too.

Now more than ever it is important to hold onto our dreams and our visions, and to remember always our star-seeded origins: that we are here in service to one another and to our planet. We must never settle for anything less than what is in our hearts. Only then can we allow our dreams to become a reality, to become our very life.

• **One Mission:** There is a saying, "Many are called, few are chosen." It really means, "All are called, many hear the call, and some actually choose to step forward and claim their divinity." All people embodied at this time have obviously said "yes" to playing their part or they simply would not be here. And we can choose ourselves in any instant when we say "yes" to our Spirit's divine plan. This truly is a magnificent time, a time for all of us to step forward and to live our own glorious spiritual truth.

So often people qualify "higher purpose," "divine work" or "spiritual mission" with a preconception of how it is supposed to look. We may not value our contribution if it doesn't look a certain way. Divine purpose is often defined as "doing" as opposed to the intent and consciousness behind the activity. In other words, it is not what we do, it is what we are. But flipping hamburgers at McDonald's is as holy and sacred a mission as leading spiritual seminars. The very breath we take is holy service. Our very existence is a sacred act. *We are the very light we seek.*

Since we are divine expressions of the Spirit of God in manifested human form, all are equal in the heart of God, for all is one. If someone quietly and joyously flips hamburgers at McDonald's, all the while loving and expressing the radiance of God presence, those who visit McDonald's will have a particularly tasty hamburger that day and not know why.

We are all beings of light and have arrived at this time for purposeful good and to play our unique part in the grand drama that is unfolding. No matter the form of entering the planet, we are all here on a sacred mission. As a species, our mission is to evolve. As individuals, our mission is to embody our Divine nature, to live and to serve as our Spirit directs. In order to discover our mission, we must become conscious, engage in all aspects of our lives, and get on about our Spirit's business.

We must steadfastly take a stand in our own spiritual truth. No matter what may happen, we must hold on unwaveringly to it. The outer circumstances of our lives will automatically begin to change and align themselves with our inner knowing. Together we will, by definition, forge a new reality. *For we are the second coming.* We have a future because we *are* the future. The wave of evolution is upon us, birthing through each of us a new world, a new species of light.

The spiral of ascension is transporting our consciousness into the oneness of our true divine, essential nature. Through the gifts of rebirth, remembrance and ascension, we are reclaiming our original state of sacred union with God presence, All That Is. We are going home, all of us.

I am a walk-in. Do I know all the future details of my life or how my purpose will manifest through me? No. No more than anyone else does, because the mystery is the adventure. I look forward to fulfilling my destiny, however it plays out.

I, like you, come to facilitate a future reality.

"For we are all one, you know. ..."

20

Information About Walk-Ins

Walk-ins are not a "phenomenon," but rather another natural expression of life. Granted, such substitutions of one soul for another may seem bizarre, but just because we may not be used to the concept does not make transformations unnatural. In the days to come many more people will wake up to the realization that they are walk-ins. Those of you who are walk-ins, who talk about your transformation experience, cut a pathway in consciousness. By so doing, you assist many others who will walk in later. They will automatically be attracted to you because your message to them will help them understand themselves and integrate who they are more gracefully.

Over the last five years, I have accumulated information about walk-ins through my own insights, through private counseling sessions with clients adjusting to walking in, through transmissions from the Council, and by comparing notes with other walk-ins. There is very little printed information on the topic, except for the seminal works of Ruth Montgomery written in the late '70s and early '80s.

I have heard stories from scores of other walk-ins about their adjustments and integration processes. I have seen the ways that such an experience affected their families and friends. There are many variations and models on the theme of the walk-in experience. Some walk-ins come in consciously, some not. Sometimes more than one walk-in experience occurs in the lifetime of the same body. Some spirits walk in during youth and only now are remembering who they are.

Though the stories vary from walk-in to walk-in, there is a very basic underlying definition that fits them all: one Spirit walks out of a body and another Spirit walks in. A completely new being is now present in human form while the original being has moved on to other assignments. Like players on a basketball team, a new player goes on to the floor to carry the ball while the previous player rotates out.

Since the walk-in experience seems unusual, people are naturally curious. When they learn who I am, they ask lots of questions. Here are the most common questions I get asked along with some actual walk-in stories of people with whom I've worked over the past five years.

What are some of the ways in which walk-ins arrive?

There are as many variations of the walk-in experience as there are walk-ins themselves. There are also many models to explain the method for Spirit exchanges such as near-death experiences, miraculous recoveries, and soul-weariness that contrast with my own experience of replacing the walk-out who completed her mission.

Near-death experience:
Ellen was in her forties, a gifted artist, a talent she

had only discovered a decade earlier, after narrowly missing death in a serious automobile accident. As a semi-truck careered head-on toward her, Ellen recognized in a split second before the impact a choice-point. Did she want to stay or to go? She experienced a calm, still void for a fraction of an instant, then a force jerked her back into her body. She swerved her car sideways to the right and drove into a ditch. The truck missed her by inches. "I know that something very unusual happened during that split second," she said, "because after that I've been an entirely different person. After that my husband seemed like a complete stranger. We divorced within two years. In that time I quit my job and changed virtually everything about my life."

Miraculous recovery:

JoAnne was a middle-aged mother of two grown sons. She was looking forward to her first grandchild and the freedom to compose a life of quiet hobbies that had been on hold while she devoted her life to motherhood. During her regular physical exam, a serious malignancy showed up on her mammogram. The doctors performed a radical mastectomy within the week. They discovered that the cancer had not only spread to her lymph nodes but throughout her body. She endured tortuous chemotherapy, with no guarantee that she would ever recover. Because JoAnne was a gentle soul, she didn't rail against the unfairness of it all. Instead, she gracefully prepared for inevitable death. After four weeks, her life force draining away, she had the unusual thought, "Hey! What's this? What's going on here?" She scanned over the sheets of the hospital bed, and out the window. "This will never do!" From that instant her body began to heal itself. Her strength ebbed back. Within two weeks she was walking up and down the hospital corridors. Within the month there was no trace of cancer anywhere in her body. Her personality changed. She became extroverted, interested in community activities. "I *know* that miracles happen," she said. "Not only am I totally cancer-free, I'm a totally different person, happier than ever before. As an activist for breast cancer research I have a stronger sense of purpose than I did even as a mother."

Soul-weariness:

Justin was in his late thirties, a well-educated investment banker who had been plagued with serious bouts of depression since childhood. After taking one type of anti-depressant drug after another, checking himself in and out of psychiatric wards, and four unsuccessful suicide attempts, he searched for *any* reason to continue his unhappy and desperate life. His soul had become so weary and fatigued that he just wanted out. Death would be such sweet relief. He collapsed on his bed overwhelmed by hope-lessness, imploring that God be merciful and take him. Finally he fell asleep, a peaceful, sound slumber without the usual fitful dozing punctuated by panic attacks. "When I awoke in the morning," he said, "it seemed like the sun was brighter and the sky was clearer than it ever had been before. I felt a strange glimmer of hope that it was possible for me to get better." Justin resolved to continue his clinical and medical therapy. After several more months he felt a growing zest for life and soon was able to function almost normally, without drugs. "I know I had a walk-in experience that night. It's amazing! I finally have the emotional resources I need to build a new life."

Mission-complete:

For a year and a half, Stephanie looked forward to a vacation from her job as a high-tech product manager. Now that her software product was released, she was finally relaxing on a white-sand beach in Hawaii, across the sea from her frenetic high-tech job and the rainy Northwest winter. As she lay under the striped beach umbrella, she looked back over her 32 years of life and felt a sense of total fulfillment and satisfaction. She had made a name for herself at her company and was surrounded by a loving and supportive family and network of close friends. A strong emotion welled up inside her, "I've done it. I'm complete. I can go now." Behind closed eyelids, somewhere off in the distance, she could sense a voice inquire matter-of-factly, "Are you ready now?" She drifted off to sleep for several hours in the warm tropical sun. When she awoke, she felt very disoriented, fumbling to recall who and where she was and how she got there. She had only a dim recollection of a dream in which someone walked out a back door and another person walked in a front door. She couldn't remember what the doors opened to, only the sense that there were two different doors and two distinct people. From that moment on her priorities shifted dramatically. She lost interest in her corporate work but stayed with her former life long enough to finish her evening studies in Chinese herbal medicine and acupuncture. "I find this work is so fulfilling. But it took me two years of questioning to realize why I had such a dramatic change in my goals and ambitions. I'm a walk-in."

What's the purpose of walking in? It seems as though there are more walk-ins now than ever before.

In these accelerated times, walking in is an efficient means of advancing mission lines to the next phase. A new team member rotates in who possesses a natural predisposition more suited for that next phase on Earth. Coming into an already-matured emotional, mental and physical body saves both time and energy. The walk-in must make some adjustments to integrate and continue the work.

Over the last couple of decades the stream of walk-ins entering the planet has been quite steady and will likely continue. It appears that there are many more walk-ins at this time because they're not only awakening to their true identities, they're talking about it more openly.

How can you tell the difference between a walk-in experience and a deep spiritual realization that changes your life?

Consciousness automatically shifts when an aspect of spiritual understanding slips past psychological or emotional awareness and lodges in a place of deep realization and knowing. Generally when people have a major shift in consciousness, or a mystical experience, they embody a fuller expression of their own Spirit. They suddenly see the world anew with new perspectives, new ideas, and new ways of identifying who they are in relationship to the world. This shift in consciousness is often facilitated by reading books and attending workshops or counseling sessions. But these are not the catalysts. They are simply tools to support their soul's divine timing and organic unfoldment into fuller awareness.

In the case of a deep consciousness change, people may demonstrate a desire for their external world to reflect the new awareness of their inner world. Even personal preferences can change when such a shift occurs. For instance, they may not care to do the things they did before, or wear the same type of clothing they wore before. They may, indeed, feel like an entirely different person. Sometimes people confuse their new sense of self-integration with a walk-in experience. They think that so much has changed for them that their Spirit must have changed too. Not so. They have had a major shift in consciousness, not an exchange of spirits. Their spiritual entity remains the same, but they are now able to live a fuller expression of it because of their expanded God-Self awareness.

Does a walk-in experience ever happen to a child? If so, why?

Absolutely. The important thing to remember is this: there are many children now being born through the normal birth process who are awake to their true identities. They come in remembering their star-seeded origins. Walk-in children are here to remind us that it's necessary for us to support these awakening children by helping them to evoke their talents and gifts so that they can expand into all that they are, and by encouraging them to stay awake through the eventual socialization process that might lull them back to sleep. As parents and guides, our job is to assist our children in learning to function here effectively, and to help them remember who they are. We must also help them express a positive discharge for all the energies that flow through them without shutting down their creativity, or over-protecting them, or over-indulging them so that they can share their gifts with the world. Of course, this also applies to *all* children, walk-ins or not.

What are some of the typical behavior traits of a walk-in?

Although I can make no generalizations here, I've noticed some characteristic responses. Right after the actual walk-in experience, there is generally some difficulty in relating to one's own history. There may be a vague sense that, "These are the people, the interests, the clothing, the home and the profession that are 'supposed to' belong in my life." The walk-in may pause for a moment to search through memory to find a link to these circumstances. Since the memories associated with the circumstance may not have the same charge as they did for the walk-out, the walk-in may feel a little more objective about them and therefore appear to others to be more detached from them and from life in general.

Walk-ins often feel an acute level of frustration and impatience in the third dimension of Earth. Frustrated with the density on this plane, they may find themselves asking questions like, "Why can't people understand the bigger picture here?" They may feel impatient because progress seems to be made so slowly. Their impatience may be expressed by a burning sense of purpose or the frustration of having no idea how to express their true selves in practical, day-to-day terms.

Walk-ins often exhibit a sudden, *dramatic* change in personality, goals, ambitions, priorities and preferences. They may even speak differently, using words and idiomatic expressions that the former inhabitants didn't use before. They may find themselves exhibiting talents, knowledge and information that they didn't express before. Unlike the natural learning and expanding process characteristic of human growth, "boom!" the transformation happens overnight, along with the unsettling experience of taking human form.

Many walk-ins speak in a direct communication style and mince no words. They just tell it like it is. It might be an efficient way to short-cut the communication process because walk-ins feel that time is compressed. It might also be because walk-ins have a strong sense of who they are. It isn't that walk-ins are insensitive to human feelings, but they may feel no need to conform to the "artificial" impediments of personal politics, or to "make nice" to help everyone else feel better about who they are. Either way, they may find themselves preferring to dispense with the set-up time of manners and protocol.

Many times walk-ins bring with them expanded awareness and clear memories of their inter-dimensional selves which are useful and efficient in their work here. They may be interested in working on the front lines of consciousness, helping to accelerate planetary awakening. And as a part of their human experience, they'll encounter the usual range of emotions and human dynamics and will likely have the usual success rates in managing those experiences, just like everyone else.

Immediately after the walk-in experience, a new soul in an established body is likely to feel an intense loneliness for a far off distant place, light years away, with vague memories of people the Spirit has left behind with absolutely no hope of ever returning to them again. Trying to explain this longing in human terms cannot approach the vastness of the Spirit's yearning to go home. The yearning may translate into coping behaviors such as an inability to relate to life and to the people here, or cutting oneself off from loved ones. It's important for the walk-in to acknowledge these strange, intense emotions but not to languish in them. In almost all cases, they dissipate over time. But yearning for home is natural for all people, walk-in or not, because we're all on a journey back to the heart of God.

Why are some walk-ins not aware that they are walk-ins?

Sometimes walk-ins will have a very vivid recollection of the actual walk-in experience. Sometimes they have no conscious awareness of the transfer. Certain people are in such social, political and economic positions that it best serves their mission for their true identity to remain anonymous, even to themselves. Revealing themselves as walk-ins could undermine their credibility or cause skepticism among people around them. The timing of their becoming

consciously aware of their walk-in status will be synchro-
nized with their spiritual awakening. As more and more
walk-ins awaken such veils will no longer be necessary.

How does one become a walk-in?

You cannot desire to be a walk-in or expect that it
will happen to you through sheer personal will. It will only
occur in the natural unfoldment of your soul's divine plan.
Sometimes people think it's glamorous, exciting or more
highly evolved to claim they are a walk-in. Walk-ins are not
in a "better-than" position. Rather, they live a natural
expression of life on Earth that is simply theirs to express.
It is not useful to hold anyone in a spiritually superior
position. It supports separateness and distorts the truth that
we are all equal and diverse in our uniqueness.

How do I know if I'm a walk-in?

Seek the information that comes from your own
knowing, your own God presence, your Spirit. All you ever
have to do is ask your Spirit to reveal to you the truth of the
matter with utmost clarity, in a manner that your logical
mind can understand. Then leave it alone. Take your attention off of the subject. In the moments when you aren't
focused on it, you'll probably find thoughts, inspirations,
even visual images dropping into your mind, that will
answer your question. You can also employ other techniques, usually closed-eyed and meditative, to allow you to
return and to remember the instant that you walked in. In
addition, there are people who have the "assignment" of
helping you to adjust and integrate the new frequencies and
to take the next steps in your mission. These people usually
can read subtle energies and can tell whether or not you are
a walk-in.

**Do walk-outs leave because they are unhappy
and can't bear their lives?**

Walk-outs rarely leave because of a relationship, or because they are unhappy. Nor do they leave because something is left undone. Quite the contrary, they usually leave simply because they completed everything they came to do psychologically, emotionally and spiritually, even though from an external point of view it might look like they "couldn't cut the mustard." Whatever the reason, it's normal for loved ones left behind to feel heart-broken, grief-stricken, baffled, abandoned and angry by the change they perceive in someone they've known and loved for years. Sometimes the remaining spouse or partner may question whether he or she wishes to remain in the relationship. They need to give themselves plenty of adjustment time to sort things out, and then follow their knowing. It doesn't serve anyone to remain in an unhappy or unsupportive relationship.

How can friends and family of the walk-in support the integration process?

Try to place no attachment or expectations upon the walk-in or to project their former "story" on them and expect the usual behaviors and responses from them. Offer loving support as the walk-in adjusts to being in the body by just holding in your thoughts that all is well. Sometimes the adjustment may be disorienting for the walk-in. It doesn't mean that something is wrong that needs to be fixed. Simply be by their side and offer your love. Allow each moment to be brand new so that all are free to discover one another anew. Actually, walk-in or not, in these times of radical shifts, people are in fact changing moment to moment. So it's useful in all relationships to allow one another to be brand new in each moment.

How long does the assimilation process for a walk-in generally take?

The assimilation process is very individual and varies from walk-in to walk-in. It's common, during the first six months, for the energies of the new entity to integrate and assimilate quite dramatically. In general, the entire process could take two to three years before the walk-in eases fully into life. The process will unfold organically, including all of the relevant experiences necessary for the soul's enrichment, however long it might take. Over time, as walk-ins become more "normal" to our awareness, and more transitional resources become available, I'm confident that the adjustment time will be accelerated.

As a walk-in, what can I do to facilitate my own integration and assimilation process?

Often, because walk-ins arrive with fresh memories of another world, subconscious programs feel dramatically misaligned. Adjustments begin immediately and sometimes rather dramatically. When a walk-in enters, it is similar to putting on a new garment. You try it on. You like the color and the style, but the sleeves are just a tad too long, one button isn't positioned perfectly and the collar is a bit wrinkled. The raw materials are all there, the basic garment, and with a few alterations it can fit perfectly.

Similarly, the walk-out's subconscious computer program will likely require a few adjustments in "karmic patterning" that form belief systems that play out in behavior patterns. These programs come from all the many life experiences, both this one and previous embodiments. Many of those programs are no longer useful and no longer support the person you are now.

There's no way to rush the integration process. And really, there's no point in it. Your Spirit has it handled, leading you into scenarios that best serve you. Simply work with third dimensional Earth life as you integrate. You can make the process more graceful by surrendering your will to control it and force it to conform to your notion of what it should be. Surrender does not mean sitting back to see what life dishes out, but rather notice what Spirit offers in front of you then actively engage with it.

As you flush up, integrate and assimilate all the vestiges of the walk-out's structures of consciousness, you can discover all the angles of the previous belief system that may still be operating in your life. Then return to your spiritual center of knowing to discern what you know to be true for you, and what you're willing to stand for as the new entity. You'll then create your own values matrix upon which to build a solid life based on your own truth.

As more and more people are awakening, more resources will become available. Seek out others with whom you are in alignment to support and assist you through the integration process.

Do all walk-ins have a special mission?

I urge you not to use the walk-in experience as a form of separation or alienation. Walk-ins are not super-human individuals. Being a walk-in doesn't make you a card-carrying member of an exclusive spiritual club. You do not occupy a grander niche in the human hierarchy of importance and social standing than anyone else.

Although your transformation may seem dramatic, unusual or unsettling, try not to treat it as odd or unique in spite of the fact that others might. Recognize that your form of service need not be superior or grandiose in any way. The light of God presence, that each person embodies, is needed in all areas of life, Therefore, there is a place for walk-ins to participate everywhere.

For example, I've met scores of walk-ins over the years. Their missions are no more "special" than anyone else's: Karie hangs wallpaper; Susan is a minister of a new-thought church; Andrew is a computer programmer; Rosie has discovered the ability to channel and offers readings for people; Thomas is a psychotherapist; Karen is a full-time mother to baby Jacob; her husband, Alex, who walked in about the same time, buys and sells rocks, minerals and gems; Russell, in his late sixties, has never been happy or comfortable with himself or his life and works at odd jobs; Elizabeth is a construction worker; Laura, who walked into a body that was paralyzed in the legs, is building a healthy body while she conducts seminars in personal and spiritual growth.

Eventually, all of us must get on about our Spirit's business. We come here to live, to love, to learn and to engage with life, expressing our unique gifts and talents. This is part of our sacred journey. Live it with joy! Because walk-in or not, none of us can afford to let the circumstances of our "birth" dictate the circumstances of our life.

Epilogue

Although winter's cold breath lulled all the trees, bushes and flowers in my garden to sleep, I nevertheless made my rounds through the yard each day, sometimes twice a day, cleaning out the old plantings and making plans for new ones. Shari's intense fondness for growing things carried over into my life and was extremely compatible with my own passion for it. She always tended a large vegetable garden and grew perfect corn and tomatoes. She enjoyed "putting up" foods for the winter, a skill she mastered early in her Amish childhood. Because food was a top priority, she never allowed herself the extravagance of growing flowers.

This garden was a gift to me and to my assimilation to life here, a supportive and nurturing place to exercise my predisposition to love the Earth. The first summer after I walked in, I attempted to tend the vegetable garden. Because I'm not inherently as interested in food as Shari was, I let it rot. I longed for the variety and gaiety of flowers. So the next season I supplanted the vegetable garden, and everywhere else in the yard, with a profusion of blossoms. I dug my hands in the dirt from first morning light to dusk.

The garden symbolized a fresh start. I loved to notice what new life popped up. Always it was the perennials, purple crocus and a host of golden daffodils. I sat right down with them, tenderly stroking their petals and fluffing up the soil around them, eye to eye with their smiling faces. I asked the Spirit of each flower for its preference of location and care and the unique essence of God presence that it radiates. For instance, the white stargazer lily, with a splash of deep pink, whispered, "I carry the essence of divine ascension. Every year I am born anew."

These flowers are living miracles. Even in the winter when their petals fade and flowers fall, appearing lifeless, I am confident that brand new blossoms will emerge every spring from their source. I am thankful for all of them and for the mysterious Universe that infuses them with life so that they might proffer their abundance. They require nothing but natural nurturing, sunlight, soil and water to repeat the miracle of birth and rebirth. There is no interruption in the flow of life. Year after year the radiant daffodil knows when to bloom. And so it is with humanity. The same universal life force flows through us all.

I love my life! I love every breath I take. I love my cosmic identity. And I love my humanness. Even though I'm living in a 45-year-old body, the identity that I now know as myself, Juelle, has only been here a short while. Yet I am now fully present, fully integrated and fully aware of my life's purpose. I look forward to the day when all people, all expressions of God, rejoice in their divine moments as well and can truly say, "I love my life!"

About The Author

Juelle "walked-in" five years ago, to a life perfectly prepared for her by the walk-out, Shari. Since then, her mission to facilitate the creation of heaven on Earth has accelerated.

Juelle is a conscious channel who acts as a third-dimensional conduit for "The Council of Twelve." She has published many magazine articles on walk-ins as well as on other topics related to practical spirituality and planetary evolution. She and her husband, Donovan, founded Light Star Mission. Together they conduct workshops as well as private counseling sessions all across North America.

Juelle creates her own heaven on Earth by hiking in the mountains, growing flowers, exploring the seashore and traveling with Donovan.

For Further Information

"The Council of Twelve" is a host of ascended masters, angelic enclaves and inter-dimensional intelligence that collectively, lovingly and compassionately illuminate the pathways home. They offer insights and inspiration to help people on Earth at this time to seek and to discover their own knowing.

If you would like to be on a mailing list to receive a newsletter, reprints of articles, audio tapes, schedules for Council meetings and workshops or for a private telephone session, please contact Juelle and Donovan at:

Light Star Mission
800-896-4954

To order additional copies of

The Walk-In

Please send ____ copies at $14.95 for each book, plus $3.50 shipping and handling for the first book, $2 for each additional book in the same order.

Enclosed is my check or money order of $_____
or [ ] Visa [ ] MasterCard

#_____ Exp. Date ____/____

Signature _____

Name _____

Street Address _____

City _____

State _____ Zip _____

Phone _____

(Advise if recipient and mailing address are different from above.)

For credit card orders call:
1-800-895-7323

or

Return this order form to:

BookPartners
P.O. Box 922
Wilsonville, OR 97070